Simple
Asian Meals

Simple
Asian Meals

IRRESISTIBLY SATISFYING AND HEALTHY DISHES

FOR THE BUSY COOK

NINA SIMONDS

RODALE

© 2012 by Nina Simonds
Photographs © 2012 by Romulo Yanes

Rodale books may be purchased for business or promotional use or for special sales. For information, please write to:
Special Markets Department, Rodale, Inc., 733 Third Avenue, New York, NY 10017

Printed in the United States of America
Rodale Inc. makes every effort to use acid-free ∞, recycled paper ♻.

Photographs by Romulo Yanes
Food styling by Paul Grimes
Prop styling by Paige Hicks
Book design by Christina Gaugler

Library of Congress Cataloging-in-Publication Data

Simonds, Nina.
    Simple Asian meals : irresistibly satisfying and healthy dishes for the busy cook / Nina Simonds.
        p.   cm.
    Includes index.
    ISBN 978-1-60529-322-6   hardcover
    1. Cooking, Asian.   2. Quick and easy cooking.   3. Cookbooks.   I. Title.
TX724.5.A1S539   2011
641.595—dc23   2011041609

Distributed to the trade by Macmillan

2   4   6   8   10   9   7   5   3   1   hardcover

RODALE

We inspire and enable people to improve their lives and the world around them.
www.rodalebooks.com

IN LOVING MEMORY OF MY MOM, WHO, LIKE MANY,
LOVED TO NURTURE BUT HAD LITTLE TIME TO COOK.
AND FOR ALL THE HOME COOKS
WHO STRIVE TO GIVE THEIR LOVED ONES
DELICIOUS, HEALTHY MEALS.

CONTENTS

INTRODUCTION

FOR A 19-YEAR-OLD college dropout who grew up in New England, traveling to Taiwan in the seventies to study food, language, and culture might have seemed like a radical thing to do. For me, it was my destiny, or so I thought when I purchased my hard-earned ticket. (I had juggled three different jobs, as an assistant baker, a pastry chef, and a sous chef, to earn the money for my passage.) It was only after boarding the plane and flying for 20 hours to the other side of the world that the reality of what I was doing actually sank in. What was I thinking?!

As it turned out, it was a fortuitous decision. I had been introduced to a Chinese surrogate family who had agreed to take me into their home. Miraculously, my Chinese mother, Mrs. Chang, turned out to be a famous cook who ran a cooking school where some of the Chinese mainland's best chefs from Taipei's finest restaurants taught their regional specialties.

By day, I was introduced to an enormous repertoire of classic banquet dishes from all over China, including crisp tea-smoked duck with ethereal steamed lotus buns, whole carp braised in a searing hot and sour sauce, and impressive hors d'oeuvre platters with slices of cooked meat and pickled vegetables shaped into ornate "Dragon Meets Phoenix" designs. I translated every recipe and meticulously recorded them in my journals. These recipes, along with the hundreds of Asian cookbooks I have collected during my numerous forays to Asia, inspired many of the dishes in the 10 cookbooks I have written through the years.

My Chinese godfather, T.C. Lai, calls these ornate dishes "food for the eyes and not for the stomach." These days I couldn't agree more. The books and recipes lie neglected, gathering dust. Those elaborate restaurant dishes no longer fuel my ideas for cooking—rather it is the home-style food that my Chinese family feasted on each night that inspires me.

The food was quite basic, but the flavors were fresh and appealing. Whereas previously I had always carefully eaten a small amount of food to maintain a svelte figure, I found that in China I could eat more and be satiated at the end of a meal. Combined with exercise, the pounds magically dropped away. I also realized it was a much healthier way to eat.

For family meals, Mrs. Chang and I purchased most of the ingredients on our pilgrimages to the local market several mornings a week. There might be a steamed fish doused with soy sauce or black vinegar and sprinkled with a touch of finely shredded ginger and scallions, or succulent, tender red-cooked spare-ribs or chicken simmered in an anise-flavored soy braising sauce. Vegetables were generally prepared simply, like a plate of stir-fried bean sprouts garnished with garlic chives, or seasonal vegetables flash-cooked with chopped garlic, salt, and rice wine. The menu changed to reflect the season and what was on hand in the kitchen. Many of the dishes were spontaneous creations.

I was particularly taken with the diverse selection of meal-in-one seafood or meat and vegetable casseroles and noodle platters that we prepared for Saturday or Sunday lunch or dinner. It is this wide-ranging assortment of simple, easy-to-prepare family dishes and meal-in-one platters that has inspired most of the recipes in this book. I've adapted classic techniques and revised ingredients to take advantage of the growing selection of prepared foods and condiments now available in supermarkets. I've also streamlined the recipes to fit my students' busy lifestyles and my own. And after many years traveling to countries all over Asia, I've broadened my repertoire to include dishes that reflect Pan-Asian influences.

In Asia, preparing the evening meal has always been a pleasure—not the chore that it has become for many multitasking working adults in this country. Indoor and outdoor market shelves are laden with mountains of vividly colored produce that evoke images of sensual watercolors, and the air is rich with the intoxicating fragrance of ripe ingredients that inspire dishes that feed family and friends.

Today, well-stocked supermarkets offer a wealth of products and ingredients that make home-cooking easier and help us make healthy and satisfying meals. Asian cooking fits seamlessly into this scenario. There are freshly cooked rotisserie chickens, an eclectic variety of quality prepared broths, precut and pre-washed vegetables, a growing variety of diverse whole grains, as well as an astounding array of spices and Asian sauces and condiments. All of this is in addition to booming farmers' markets that offer gorgeous, freshly picked produce.

You'll notice that after many of the recipes, I have highlighted selected ingredients in the dish and listed their health-giving properties according to traditional Chinese medicine and scientific research. This reflects my keen interest in eating food that's healthy and delicious, a way of thinking that was ingrained in me from the beginning of my time in Asia. The Chinese have always embraced the idea of "food as medicine," a topic I explored in depth in two of my previous books, *A Spoonful of Ginger* (Knopf, 1999) and *Spices of Life* (Knopf, 2005). It is a way of thinking and cooking that I still feel passionately about to this day. Chinese chefs and Asian cooks integrate this idea into all their food, whether it is simpler home-cooked dishes or more elaborate banquet fare.

Home cooking isn't fancy, but, as I discovered, it's the food that nurtures. Many years later, after traveling to countries all over Asia and feasting on innumerable local delicacies, the banquet meals have become a blur while so many of the humbler dishes remain memorable. It is these foods that I have sought to adapt and recreate, and that have inspired most of the food in this book. It is my hope that the recipes will lure cooks into the kitchen by introducing them to more accessible, yet irresistible, Asian-inspired dishes and that they will dispel the myth that Asian cooking is too time-consuming and difficult to prepare on a daily basis.

THE NEW ASIAN PANTRY

WHEN I FIRST started writing about Chinese and Asian cooking in *Gourmet* magazine more than 30 years ago, the mainstream supermarket was a very different place. A trip to an Asian specialty market was a necessity in order to purchase the basic Asian condiments and produce to make most of the recipes.

Fortunately this is no longer the case: "international" aisles in today's supermarkets offer a great selection of basic Chinese, Thai, Japanese, Vietnamese, and Indian sauces and spices. Produce aisles are chock full of fat knobs of fresh ginger, stalks of lemongrass, and selected Asian vegetables, and freshly made wontons and noodles—not to mention the amazing array of tofu products—are easy to find.

So the good news is that while it is helpful to have a pantry stocked with a few prime Asian ingredients, if you need to run out to purchase any, you won't have to drive far. Below is a list of staple items to have on hand when preparing many of the recipes in this book.

While the basic ingredients with some suggested substitutions are listed here, feel free to improvise if necessary. Most of the bottled condiments and spices will keep for a year, some indefinitely when stored in a cool, dry place. Once opened, pastes, sauces, and other perishable items should be stored in the refrigerator and some transferred to tightly sealed containers.

I highly recommend buying organic meats, fruits, and vegetables. They usually cost more, but they taste better. Also, new evidence suggests that the levels of certain nutrients may be higher in organically grown foods. And I recommend free-range meats, which are usually free of hormones, antibiotics, and artificial growth enhancers.

Chicken broth: Use free-range or organic chicken broth, preferably low-sodium, in cardboard containers. Unopened, it will keep for months (check the "sell by" date). Store in a cool, dry place.

Dried chili peppers and/or **chili flakes:** These days, I tend to substitute dried red chili pepper flakes (also labelled crushed red peppers) for dried red peppers. If you are using whole dried peppers, remember that the smaller the pepper, the more intense the heat. Store them in a cool, dry place, tightly wrapped in plastic bags.

Five-spice powder: This fragrant mixture, generally used to flavor sauces and marinades, is made with a blend of spices that varies depending on the manufacturer. The usual seasonings are star anise and/or powdered licorice root, cinnamon, Sichuan peppercorns, cloves, and fennel.

Garlic chili paste: These days I alternate using chili paste and dried red pepper flakes, often substituting one for the other. I recommend buying either sambal olek or the Vietnamese chili paste with the rooster on the label. Once opened, store in the refrigerator. Sriracha hot sauce is also a substitute.

Garlic, fresh ginger (gingerroot), and **red onions:** I usually prefer the flavor (sweeter) and color of red onions. Since I use ginger quite frequently, I store it with my other seasonings in a basket on the counter. While some cooks recommend storing ginger in rice wine, it will cause the ginger to disintegrate. Freezing ginger often causes the same effect.

   Tip: Bury ginger (and other root herbs) in a pot of sand and it will keep on your counter indefinitely.

Grains: A good selection includes white or brown basmati or jasmine rice, quick-cooking whole wheat, plain, or tri-color couscous, and quinoa and quinoa mixes.

Herbs and **spices:** A good selection includes dried basil, black pepper, cumin, curry powder, cinnamon, cloves, coriander, garlic, oregano, ground ginger, nutmeg, and turmeric. A good online source is www.thespicehouse.com.

Tips: Store spices in a cool, dry place away from heat. Replace every few years since they tend to become less fragrant and flavorful. Toast briefly in a dry, hot skillet to refresh.

Hoisin sauce: Ground bean sauces such as hoisin are found in various forms all over China. This southern version is made with fermented beans, salt, sugar, and garlic. Its primary uses are in marinades for barbecuing and roasting and in dipping sauces. Store it in the refrigerator and it will keep indefinitely. Lee Kum Kee makes an acceptable hoisin, but the best brand is Koon Chun.

Oils: Stock your pantry with two types of *extra-virgin* olive oil: The first, which is relatively inexpensive and comes in a big bottle (Colavita, Trader Joe's, and Whole Foods brands are recommended), is excellent for frying and general cooking. The other oil, which is fruity, more expensive, and comes in a smaller bottle, can be used for making dressings for pasta and cold dishes. Olive oil helps to lower cholesterol and blood pressure and prevent heart disease. Canola, soy, sunflower, and peanut oil are beneficial as well and smoke at higher temperatures, so they are good for frying.

Oyster sauce: Lustrous and rich, oyster sauce is a concentrated mixture made from fermented oysters, salt, and assorted seasonings. It is especially appropriate for seafood and vegetable dishes. Once opened, it will keep indefinitely in the refrigerator. Lee Kum Kee makes the best brand.

Rice wine/sake or **dry vermouth:** Rice wine (also known as sake) is an all-purpose Chinese wine that is used in cooking or consumed as a beverage. I like to use it in sauces or to stir-fry vegetables. It is commonly available where wine and spirits are sold. The Gekkeikan brand is recommended. Substitute with a very dry and high-quality sherry or a dry white wine.

Sesame oil (toasted): Asian sesame oil is made from roasted sesame seeds; it is not interchangeable with the pressed sesame oil found in health foods stores. Buy the Roland, Kame, or Kadoya brands.

Soy sauce: Naturally brewed Japanese soy sauce is found in most supermarkets and is appropriate for all dishes. Use all-purpose soy or a light version (less salty) as needed. My favorite is Kikkoman, manufactured in Japan and sold in Asian markets.

Vinegars: Good-quality **balsamic** and **rice wine vinegar** are good to have on hand. Clear rice wine vinegar is lighter and slightly sweeter than most fruit-based vinegars, so it is advisable to have some. I recommend using the Marukan unflavored green label rice vinegar. For a substitute, dilute cider vinegar in equal parts water and use as directed. **Chinese black vinegar** is often used in sauces, dressings, and dips. The best and, to my mind, only brand to use is Chinkiang, which is sold in Asian markets. Although the flavor is not exactly the same, Worcestershire sauce is the best substitute.

TIPS FOR WEEKNIGHT COOKING

THIS BOOK IS all about convenience, enjoyment, and health. By using many of the quality convenience and prepared foods now available in the supermarket, it's possible to reduce the preparation time of many dishes without sacrificing quality or flavor. Accordingly, I've devised these recipes to be as easy, flavorful, fast, and accessible as possible.

As the recipes in this book readily demonstrate, cooking Asian food does not need to be labor intensive, nor does it require special shopping trips (or ordering from online specialty food purveyors). Most of the dishes are meals in themselves and use ingredients available at most well-stocked large supermarkets. Here are some suggestions that may also help you to make these meals a spontaneous weeknight event:

- Stock your pantry with the Asian staples normally called for in the recipes, such as soy sauce, rice wine or sake, rice vinegar, toasted sesame oil, and fresh ginger mentioned in The New Asian Pantry (page xiii).

- Keep on hand other basic items like roasted red peppers, a good selection of whole grains and rice such as jasmine or brown and white basmati rice, quinoa, and whole wheat couscous, as well as a selection of Asian and Western noodles such as Chinese or Thai rice stick noodles, soba, angel hair, and whole wheat pasta, and a good quality extra-virgin olive oil.

- Use the weekend to shop and to plan meals.

- Prepare large batches of staples like rice and other grains for freezing in individual bags and defrosting when needed the day of the meal.

- Mince ¼ cup of chopped garlic and ginger and store in plastic bags to keep on hand in the refrigerator for use during the week.

- Make large batches of marinades or spice rubs to have available for seasoning meat, seafood, or tofu before grilling or roasting.

- Try using quality prepared foods from the markets such as rotisserie chickens, rinsed and cut vegetables, and slaws to shorten meal preparation time.

- Prepare large portions of stir-fried, roasted, and grilled meats, seafood, and vegetables on weekends to use for dinners during the week.

- Review each recipe and prepare sauces, minced seasonings, and marinades before cooking.

- Relax, take a deep breath, and have a glass of wine or beer while preparing the food. Learn to consider the time spent cooking dinner as a period for reflection and decompressing rather than as a chore. (Try some shoulder rolls and stretches between prepping the ingredients and cooking the food.)

- Encourage members of your family or household to help with the meal preparation. Make a list, share the "work," and use the time to catch up.

- Make every evening meal a daily ritual and a celebration that allows family members to get together and talk, unwind, and enjoy one another's company.

WARMING AND COOLING FOODS

YIN AND YANG represent the opposing yet complementary forces of the universe and the Chinese believe that everything is influenced by their ebb and flow. According to one of the most basic beliefs in Chinese medicine, disease occurs due to an imbalance of yin and yang in the body and food can help to maintain that balance, thereby preventing disease. Everyone's body possesses both yin (cold) and yang (hot) elements, but you may be more predisposed toward one or the other depending on your age, health, lifestyle, environment, and diet.

The best and most reliable way to find out whether you are yin or yang is to visit a qualified Chinese doctor, but in general, those who are dominated by too much yin tend to be thin and pale-faced, sensitive to cold, listless, and lacking energy. Conversely those with a preponderance of yang tend to be heavyset or overweight, not sensitive to cold, and easily constipated.

All foods are divided into three categories: warming, cooling, and neutral, depending on their effect on the body. Yin or cooling foods such as fruits, vegetables, and many types of seafood, are recommended to offset too much yang. Yang or warming foods, which include beef, lamb, eggs, and hot spices, are eaten to counterbalance too much yin. Neutral foods provide balance.

The body often craves the foods it needs as well as those available according to the natural order of the seasons: In the summer, when it is hot (yang) we crave yin foods, like salads, nonspicy soups, melons, bean dishes, mung beans, sprouts, sushi, nonspicy soups, and lots of water. In the winter or cooler weather, we crave yang foods like hearty stews and soups made with meat and root vegetables, oily and heavier dishes. Neutral foods can be eaten at any time throughout the year, and these include brown and white rice, breads, and noodles.

✄

HEARTY SOUP POTS

HEARTY SOUP POTS

I'VE ALWAYS THOUGHT of soups as nurturing and comforting, even as a child. But it wasn't until I lived in Asia that I was introduced to the extraordinary diversity and exciting nuances of the flavors and textures of Asian soups—not to mention their numerous health-giving benefits. Furthermore, with minimal fuss and some staple ingredients, soups can provide infinite pleasure and a filling meal-in-one dish.

Years ago, at a little cooking school I attended in Taipei, the Chinese master chefs taught me the more refined and elaborate soups of Chinese haute cuisine (including shark's fin and bird's nest). But, as I discovered when I cooked the nightly dinner meal or Sunday lunch with my surrogate Chinese mother, it was the simpler, seasonal, home-style soups—like Home-Style Chicken Ginger Soup with Bok Choy and Sumptuous Hot and Sour Vegetable Soup—that were so satisfying and memorable.

Since I was a student with limited means, my schoolmates and I would frequent the inexpensive noodle stalls that lined the street where I studied Mandarin. One of our favorite haunts—especially during the raw, cold winter of my first year in Taipei—was Earl's Noodles, where Chef Chang cooked an intoxicatingly delicious bowl of Cinnamon Beef Noodles. Nothing comforted me more when I was hungry, homesick, or chilled to the bone than a large bowl of those sumptuous noodles in broth, topped with pieces of tender, soy-braised meat and some crisp-tender green vegetables. To this day, it is equally appealing, and my husband and son have also become big fans.

Years later, when my busy schedule limited my prep time for family meals, I discovered that many of the soup recipes I had gathered while traveling in Asia could be easily streamlined and adapted without sacrificing their sumptuous flavors. In this chapter, I present a number of my tried-and-true favorites. Most are single-dish meals by themselves.

Because I traveled extensively throughout Asia, there are soups from many different countries: While I was writing a book on noodles (and traveling extensively through Japan), my husband and I have become addicted to the nutty flavor of buckwheat (or soba) noodles in *dashi*, an enticingly smoky stock. Forays to Vietnam introduced me to Saigon-style pho, a celebrated soup made with star anise and cinnamon-flavored chicken cooked in broth with rice noodles; Soothing Saigon-Style Chicken Noodle Soup is my version of this hearty soup. Vietnam also introduced me to Hot and Sour Shrimp Soup seasoned with lemongrass, lime juice, and crushed chile pepper. Both soups are sprinkled with herbs like cilantro, basil, and chopped scallions at the last moment, adding an irresistible burst of freshness.

My surrogate Chinese mother and the Chinese chefs I studied under always *insisted* that a good soup had to be made with a stock from scratch, and, for many years, this was my mantra as well. But that was before supermarkets started offering good-quality organic and free-range broths in cartons. Infusing the broth briefly with several slices of smashed fresh ginger and a bit of rice wine (or sake) transforms it into a surprisingly delicious, homemade-tasting base. Other shortcuts include using peeled garlic, precut vegetables, and a food processor to chop and slice ingredients.

This chapter offers a selection of my favorite Asian soups. Some are old favorites; others are new creations. The majority of the recipes are meal-in-one noodle pots, and the rest may be served with crusty bread or whole grains to round out the meal. Variations are offered after most recipes, but don't be afraid to improvise, using what's available or seasonal. I like to make big pots of the basic stock and freeze it in batches. Once defrosted and heated and with the addition of freshly cooked vegetables, meat or seafood, and noodles, they become a comforting and nourishing meal in minutes.

EFFORTLESS CHINESE CHICKEN STOCK

MAKES 6 CUPS

Making soup used to be a labor of love, but with the introduction of organic and free-range broths in the supermarket, the labor is not a necessity. It takes only minutes to doctor these flavorful store-bought stocks with a bit of fresh ginger and rice wine to make them taste uncannily like they have been cooking for hours.

1 carton (1 quart) store-bought chicken broth, preferably low-sodium

1 1/2 cups water

1/2 cup rice wine or sake

6 slices fresh ginger about the size of a quarter, smashed lightly with the flat side of a knife or cleaver

Combine the chicken broth, water, rice wine, and ginger in a large saucepan and bring to a boil. Reduce the heat and simmer uncovered for 15 minutes. Use a slotted spoon to fish out the ginger and discard.

> Chicken broth, particularly when it's made with an organic or natural (hormone-free) chicken, is an ideal medium for numerous soups. Chicken is warming and acts as a *qi* (or energy) tonic. The broth also aids digestion.

BASIC JAPANESE STOCK (*DASHI*)

MAKES ABOUT 8 CUPS

Dashi is a simple stock that forms the base of many Japanese soups. The flavor is enticingly smoky and it takes only minutes to prepare. The two key ingredients, kelp and bonito shavings, are available in the international section of most supermarkets and health food stores, and in Asian markets. Both ingredients will keep indefinitely in the pantry when wrapped tightly in plastic.

One 4-inch square kelp (*kombu*), wiped clean with a damp cloth

½ cup (about 6 grams) dried bonito flakes

8 cups water

1. Place the kelp and water in a large pot. Bring to a boil, then immediately remove the kelp with tongs. Set aside for another use or discard.

2. Add the bonito flakes, stir well, and remove the pot from the heat. Let the flakes settle to the bottom of the pot (about 1 minute), then pour the stock through a fine strainer or a coarse strainer lined with cheesecloth.

> In addition to providing numerous minerals, vitamins, and amino acids, seaweeds (such as kelp) are an excellent source of iodine, calcium, and iron. Kombu, a member of the kelp family, provides moisture in the body and improves kidney function.

SUMPTUOUS HOT AND SOUR VEGETABLE SOUP

6 TO 8 SERVINGS

Nothing could be more satisfying or warming than a bowl of hot and sour soup. Traditionally, the soup is made with pork, but I prefer to use chicken. Buy preshredded vegetables to save time, and add any leftover vegetables you may have on hand. This soup is one of those dishes that increases in flavor when reheated.

1 small head Napa cabbage (about 1½ pounds)

2 large leeks (about 1 pound), white and light green parts only, sliced lengthwise, rinsed, and drained

1½ tablespoons olive or canola oil

2½ tablespoons peeled and minced fresh ginger

6 to 8 ounces fresh shiitake mushrooms, stemmed and thinly sliced

¼ cup rice wine or sake

14 ounces very firm tofu, halved crosswise and each half cut crosswise into ¼-inch slices

8 cups or 2 cartons (32 ounces each) chicken or vegetable broth, preferably low-sodium

2½ tablespoons cornstarch mixed with ¼ cup water

4½ tablespoons Chinese black vinegar or Worcestershire sauce, or more to taste

3 tablespoons soy sauce, or to taste

1 teaspoon toasted sesame oil

1 teaspoon salt, or to taste

¾ teaspoon freshly ground black pepper

1 large egg, lightly beaten

1. Cut away the stem of the cabbage and discard. Cut the cabbage lengthwise in half, then cut each half lengthwise in half again. Cut each quarter into 1½-inch sections, separating the leafy sections from the stem pieces, and place in a bowl. Cut each leek half into thin slices, about ¼ inch thick. Prepare all the remaining ingredients and place near the stove.

2. Heat the oil in a large, heavy pot over medium-high heat until hot, about 25 seconds. Add the leeks and ginger and stir-fry until fragrant, about 15 seconds. Add the tougher sections of the cabbage and the mushrooms and toss lightly for 1 to 2 minutes, until slightly softened.

3. Add the rice wine, partially cover, and reduce the heat slightly. Cook for about 5 minutes, until tender and dry. Add the leafier sections of the cabbage, the tofu slices, and the broth and bring to a boil. Lower the heat slightly and simmer for 15 minutes.

(continued)

4. Slowly add the cornstarch and water mixture, stirring constantly to prevent lumps. Cook over medium-high heat until the broth has thickened, 3 to 4 minutes. The soup should have the consistency of heavy cream. Stir in the black vinegar, soy sauce, sesame oil, salt, and black pepper; taste for seasoning, adding more soy sauce if necessary. Turn off the heat and slowly add the egg, pouring it in a thin stream around the circumference of the pot. Stir the soup several times. Ladle the hot soup into bowls, and serve immediately.

VARIATIONS: *Add 1 cup shredded carrots for extra color and 1 teaspoon crushed red pepper flakes for additional spiciness.*

Substitute 6 to 8 dried black mushrooms or 1¼ ounces dried porcini mushrooms for the fresh shiitakes. Rinse and soften in hot water to cover, reserving the broth. (You can extend the broth with additional water and use in place of vegetable broth or add to chicken broth for extra flavor.) Trim the mushroom stems or tough ends, discard, and use the caps as above.

> Shiitake mushrooms have a smoky, meaty flavor and are believed to strengthen the immune system and prevent tumors. They may also prevent heart disease by lowering cholesterol.

HEARTY MISO–BEAN CURD SOUP
WITH SWISS CHARD

6 SERVINGS

Whereas miso paste was once available only in Asian specialty markets, it is now sold in mainstream supermarkets alongside the other tofu products. Adding just $1/3$ cup to the stock can transform it into a delectable base that's perfect for cooked vegetables, meats, seafood, or tofu. Miso varies widely in flavor and saltiness depending on the brand. You may have to add a little more, depending on your palate.

8 cups Basic Japanese Stock (page 5) or Effortless Chinese Chicken Stock (page 4)

2 squares firm or soft tofu (about 1½ pounds), cut into thin slices about ¼ inch thick and 1½ inches long

1 bunch Swiss chard (about 1 pound), rinsed, center ribs and stems discarded, leaves coarsely chopped (about 5 cups)

⅓ cup sweet white miso paste (*miso shiro*), or more to taste

3½ tablespoons chopped scallion greens

1. Bring the stock to a boil in a large soup pot. Add the tofu slices and chard leaves and partially cover. When the stock reaches a boil, reduce the heat to medium, uncover, and cook for 2 to 3 minutes, until the chard leaves are nearly tender.

2. Place the miso paste in a small bowl. Add about ¼ cup of the hot stock and mix to a smooth paste. Add a little more broth to smooth out the paste, then stir the mixture into the soup. Add the scallion greens and stir. Taste the soup for seasoning, adding additional miso paste if needed, but dissolving it first in a little broth. Serve immediately.

VARIATIONS: *For the chard, substitute other leafy vegetables such as spinach, Napa cabbage, kale, or watercress, cooking them until they are tender.*

Add other vegetables for extra flavor and color, such as sliced shiitake or other mushrooms, carrots, shelled edamame, peas, or snow or snap peas.

Miso is packed with health-giving nutrients, the Japanese credit it with promoting long life and good health by strengthening the body's resistance to disease. It is a great source of protein and, similar to yogurt, contains lactobacillus, live bacteria that aid digestion.

FIVE-SPICE CARROT SOUP WITH GINGERY SNAP PEAS

6 TO 8 SERVINGS

This velvety-rich soup takes almost no time to cook, and the flavor can be subtly altered with the addition of different spices. I like to add a hint of ginger and a whisper of five-spice powder, but nutmeg or cumin is also delicious. Served with crusty bread, it's an easy and filling meal.

One 1-inch knob peeled fresh ginger or 3 1/2 tablespoons chopped ginger

1 pound onions, peeled and quartered

3 1/2 tablespoons olive or canola oil

1 1/2 pounds baby carrots

7 cups low-sodium chicken broth

1/2 teaspoon five-spice powder

1 1/2 teaspoons salt

1/4 teaspoon freshly ground black pepper

3/4 pound snap peas or snow peas, ends snapped and strings removed

2 tablespoons rice wine or sake

1. In a blender or a food processor fitted with a steel blade, pulse to finely chop the ginger. Add the onions and continue pulsing until coarsely chopped.

2. Heat 3 tablespoons of the oil in a heavy large pot over medium heat until hot. Add about 1 tablespoon of the chopped ginger and the onions and stir-fry for about 15 seconds, until very fragrant. Cover and cook for 2 to 3 minutes, until the onions are transparent. Add the carrots and broth and bring to boil. Reduce the heat to medium-low and simmer, partially covered, until the carrots are tender, 25 to 30 minutes.

3. Using a Chinese wire strainer, remove the carrots from the broth and place in a bowl to cool slightly. Working in batches, puree the carrots in the food processor or blender until smooth, adding 1/2 cup of the broth to each batch. Return the pureed carrots and broth to the pot and reheat, seasoning with the five-spice powder, 1 teaspoon salt, and the pepper.

4. While the soup is reheating, heat the remaining 1/2 tablespoon oil over high heat in a heavy skillet or wok. When hot, add the snow or snap peas, the remaining chopped ginger, the rice wine, and the remaining 1/2 teaspoon salt. Stir-fry for about 2 minutes, until the peas are crisp-tender, and remove to a plate. To serve, either stir the peas into the carrot soup or ladle soup into bowls and sprinkle the peas on top. Serve hot.

VARIATION: *Substitute 1 teaspoon ground cumin or 1 1/2 teaspoons curry powder (or to taste) for the five-spice powder.*

DELICATE SHRIMP AND ASPARAGUS IN CHICKEN BROTH

6 SERVINGS

Eastern Chinese soups are renowned for their delicacy, and this soup is a fine example. The flavoring is subtle, accentuating the fresh true tastes of the ingredients. It's a light but filling meal. Traditionally, thin Amoy-style flour-and-water noodles are used, but Japanese somen or angel hair noodles can be substituted.

1 pound raw medium shrimp, peeled, deveined, rinsed, and drained

3 tablespoons rice wine or sake

1½ tablespoons minced fresh ginger

½ teaspoon toasted sesame oil

6 ounces thin Chinese amoy noodles or angel hair noodles

1 teaspoon olive or canola oil

¼ cup minced scallions

1 tablespoon minced garlic

6 cups Effortless Chinese Chicken Stock (page 4) or water

1 pound asparagus, tough woody ends discarded and cut into 2-inch pieces

1 teaspoon salt, or to taste

2 to 3 tablespoons fresh lemon juice

1. Cut the shrimp lengthwise along the back and place in a bowl. Add the rice wine, ginger, and sesame oil, tossing to coat. Set aside to marinate while you prepare the soup.

2. Bring a large pot of water to a boil. Add the noodles and cook for a little less time than the package instructions indicate, until just tender. Drain in a colander and rinse under warm water. Drain and divide the cooked noodles evenly among 6 serving bowls.

3. Heat a heavy soup pot over high heat until hot. Add the oil and heat for about 20 seconds, until very hot. Add the scallions and garlic and stir-fry for 15 seconds, until fragrant. Add the chicken stock and bring nearly to a boil, then add the asparagus. Reduce the heat to medium and simmer for about 6 minutes. Add the shrimp and continue cooking at a simmer for 2 minutes, or until the shrimp turn pink, skimming the broth to remove any foam or impurities. Add the salt and lemon juice. Taste for seasoning and adjust if necessary. Ladle the soup over the noodles and serve immediately.

VARIATIONS: *For extra flavor, add ½ teaspoon crushed red pepper flakes and/or 1½ teaspoons (or to taste) good-quality curry powder with the ginger.*

Substitute spinach, split and blanched baby bok choy, snow peas, or snow pea shoots for the asparagus and cook until crisp-tender.

FIERY VIETNAMESE HOT AND SOUR SHRIMP SOUP

6 SERVINGS

Lemongrass, chilis, fresh lime juice, and cilantro are among the vibrant seasonings used by Vietnamese cooks to create their memorable specialties. Plump shrimp, crisp bean sprouts, and silken noodles help to create a delightful contrast of flavors in this soup. Savor and enjoy.

3 stalks lemongrass, tough outer stalks removed and ends trimmed (use the central, tender section of the stalk)

1 teaspoon olive or canola oil

3 shallots, chopped (about $\frac{1}{4}$ cup)

1 scant teaspoon crushed red pepper flakes, or to taste

3 medium vine-ripened tomatoes, cored, seeded, and coarsely chopped

6 to 8 ounces button mushrooms, thinly sliced

6 cups water

1 pound raw medium shrimp, peeled, halved horizontally, deveined, rinsed, and drained

5 $\frac{1}{2}$ tablespoons Thai fish sauce

3 $\frac{1}{2}$ tablespoons fresh lime juice

1 $\frac{1}{2}$ ounces cellophane noodles, softened for 10 minutes in boiling hot water and drained

3 $\frac{1}{2}$ cups bean sprouts, rinsed and drained

3 tablespoons chopped fresh cilantro leaves

1. Cut each lemongrass stalk lengthwise in half and smash with the flat edge of a knife.

2. Heat the oil in a heavy non-aluminum pot over medium-high heat until hot. Add the lemongrass, shallots, and crushed red pepper and stir-fry until fragrant, about 15 seconds. Add the tomatoes and mushrooms and continue stir-frying for about a minute. Add the water, bring to a boil, then reduce the heat to low. Simmer, partially covered, for about 3 minutes.

3. Increase the heat slightly. Add the shrimp, fish sauce, lime juice, and drained cellophane noodles. Simmer for about 3 minutes, until the shrimp are nearly cooked and the cellophane noodles are tender. Use tongs to remove the lemongrass and discard. Stir in the bean sprouts and cilantro and cook for a minute, until heated through, skimming the surface to remove any impurities. Taste and adjust the seasoning, adding more fish sauce if necessary. Serve immediately.

Unlike most seafood, shrimp are warming to the body.
Chinese believe that they increase *qi* energy.

NUTTY SOBA NOODLE POT
WITH CHICKEN AND SCALLIONS

6 SERVINGS

One taste of this soothing soup and I am transported back to the Kanda Yabu Soba restaurant in Tokyo, where soba noodles are still made by hand, as they have been since 1860. This is my simplified, yet no less delicious, version of its refined classic. It's one of my family's staple meals for a weeknight dinner, and the dish reheats beautifully.

1¼ pounds boneless, skinless chicken breasts

3 tablespoons rice wine or sake

8 ounces soba noodles

1½ teaspoons olive or canola oil

8 whole scallions, trimmed and chopped

1½ tablespoons minced garlic

8 cups chicken broth, preferably low-sodium, or Basic Japanese Stock (page 5)

3 tablespoons soy sauce, plus more to taste

7 to 8 ounces baby spinach, well-rinsed (shredded Swiss chard, kale, or Napa cabbage can be substituted)

2 teaspoons toasted sesame oil

1. Using a sharp knife, cut the chicken crosswise into thin slices about ¼ inch thick. Place the chicken in a bowl, add the rice wine, toss lightly to coat, and set aside.

2. Bring a large pot of water to a boil. Add the soba noodles, return to a boil, and cook for 3 to 3½ minutes, until al dente or nearly tender. Drain and rinse under warm running water. Divide the noodles evenly among 6 soup bowls.

3. Heat the oil in a casserole dish or Dutch oven over high heat until hot. Add the chopped scallions and garlic and stir-fry until fragrant, about 20 seconds. Add the chicken broth and soy sauce and bring to a gentle boil over medium heat. Add the chicken slices and cook for 5 to 6 minutes, until almost cooked completely, skimming any foam or impurities from the surface. Stir in the spinach leaves and sesame oil, cover the pot, and cook for about a minute, until the leaves are just wilted. Taste for seasoning, adding more soy sauce if necessary.

4. Ladle the chicken, spinach, and hot broth over the noodles and serve immediately.

> Soba noodles are made with varying amounts of buckwheat and wheat flour. They are rich in protein and dietary fiber, which helps to lower cholesterol and promote regularity.

ASIAN FISH CHOWDER WITH FRESH BASIL

6 SERVINGS

Cream-based fish chowders can be heavy and lumpy, but this Asian-inspired chowder has a light chicken stock base and is chock full of plump poached cod complemented by slices of fennel and fresh basil. I like to ladle it over noodles, but you could also serve it with a loaf of crusty bread.

1½ pounds firm-fleshed fish fillets such as cod, sea bass, halibut, or red snapper, skin removed

6 slices fresh ginger, smashed with the flat side of a knife

3 tablespoons plus ½ cup rice wine or sake

8 ounces somen, angel hair, or other thin noodles

1½ teaspoons olive or canola oil

3 tablespoons chopped garlic (about 8 cloves)

½ cup chopped scallions (3 to 4 scallions)

6 cups Effortless Chinese Chicken Stock (page 4) or chicken broth, preferably low-sodium

2 large fennel bulbs (about 1½ pounds), trim stalks and root base, leaving bulb with ⅛ inch of stem; cut in half lengthwise and turn cut side down; slice into ¼-inch-thick pieces

¾ cup Thai holy basil or sweet basil leaves, chopped or finely shredded

3 tablespoons fresh lemon juice

2 tablespoons Thai fish sauce

½ teaspoon freshly ground black pepper

1. Using a sharp knife, cut the fish into chunks, about 1½ inches square. Place the fish in a bowl, add the ginger and the 3 tablespoons rice wine, and toss lightly to coat.

2. Bring 3 quarts of water to a boil, add the noodles, and cook until near tender or al dente. Drain in a colander and rinse under warm running water. Divide the noodles among 6 soup bowls.

3. Heat the oil in a large soup pot over high heat until hot, about 20 seconds. Add the garlic and scallions and stir-fry until fragrant, about 15 seconds. Add the chicken stock and the remaining ½ cup rice wine and bring to a boil. Reduce the heat to medium, add the fennel, and partially cover the pot. Cook for 10 to 12 minutes, until the fennel is almost tender. Discard the ginger slices. Add the fish chunks with the marinade to the pot. Cover and cook for 5 to 6 minutes, until the fish pieces flake when prodded with a knife.

4. Add the fresh basil, lemon juice, fish sauce, and black pepper to the soup and stir gently to marry the flavors. Taste for seasoning, adding more fish sauce if it needs salt. Ladle the soup over the noodles and serve.

VARIATION: *Substitute striped bass, tilapia, haddock, shrimp, or scallops for the cod, cooking the fish until flaky, and the shrimp or scallops until firm and completely cooked.*

HOME-STYLE CHICKEN GINGER SOUP WITH BOK CHOY

6 SERVINGS

This soup was a cold-weather staple in my Chinese family's home. It's so easy to make, yet so nurturing. I like to make a huge pot, then freeze it in batches to reheat for a hearty lunch or dinner, adding other leftover bits of cooked vegetables from the refrigerator with each reheating.

1 small head Chinese bok choy, or 1 bunch baby bok choy (about 1 1/2 pounds)

1 1/2 pounds boneless, skinless chicken thighs, trimmed of fat and gristle

5 to 6 ounces rice stick noodles or vermicelli, soaked in boiling water for 10 minutes and drained (optional)

2 teaspoons olive or canola oil

2 tablespoons minced garlic

2 1/2 tablespoons chopped fresh ginger

4 to 6 ounces fresh shiitake or cremini mushrooms, stemmed and thinly sliced

1/2 cup rice wine or sake

6 cups chicken broth, preferably low-sodium

3 tablespoons fresh lemon juice

2 tablespoons soy sauce, plus more to taste

1. Remove any tough or wilted outer stalks from the bok choy and discard. Using a sharp knife, trim both ends of the stalks, discarding an inch of the leafy section and any other wilted leaves. Put the bok choy in the sink in water to cover and rinse thoroughly, since it is often sandy. Drain thoroughly. Slice the stalks crosswise about 1/4 inch thick. Cut the leafy sections into 1/2-inch pieces, keeping the leafy sections separate from the stems.

2. Using a sharp knife, cut the chicken into 1-inch pieces and set aside. If using the rice noodles, cook the soaked noodles in boiling water for 1 minute, or until tender. Drain and rinse under warm running water. Drain again and divide among 6 serving bowls.

3. Heat the oil in a large pot over medium-high heat. When very hot, add the stalk sections of the bok choy, the garlic, ginger, and mushrooms. Stir-fry for a minute. Stir in the rice wine,

reduce the heat slightly, and cook, partially covered, for 2 minutes. Add the chicken broth and bring to a boil. Add the chicken pieces, stir to separate, and reduce the heat. Simmer uncovered for 5 to 6 minutes, until the chicken is almost cooked, skimming the surface to remove any impurities. Add the leafy green section of the bok choy and cook, partially covered, for 2 minutes. Add the lemon juice and soy sauce and taste for seasoning, adding more soy sauce if necessary.

4. Ladle the chicken soup over the rice noodles and serve.

VARIATIONS: *Use spinach, snow peas, baby cabbage hearts, or other members of the cabbage family instead of the bok choy.*

Substitute slices of flavored, baked tofu, such as teriyaki, for the chicken.

For additional flavor, mix some of the broth with ⅓ cup sweet white miso paste (miso shiro) *or 2 teaspoons curry powder and add to the soup.*

Chicken is considered one of the ultimate *qi*, or energy, tonics, and can increase the body's basic vitality, resistance to disease, and longevity. It is also warming to the body and can help improve digestion. Ideally, use natural or organic chickens that have been raised without hormones, antibiotics, or chemicals.

CURRY-COCONUT CHICKEN CASSEROLE

6 SERVINGS

Chicken soup has many wonderful variations, but the combination of chicken, coconut, and curry is extraordinarily rich and satisfying. I like to make a large pot and then add different vegetables for subsequent meals. One night I'll defrost it and add green beans, and the next night I'll toss in roasted sweet potatoes and/or tofu.

2½ tablespoons olive or canola oil

1 large red onion, finely chopped (about 2 cups)

2 tablespoons minced fresh ginger

2 tablespoons good-quality Madras curry powder

1 scant teaspoon crushed red pepper flakes, or to taste

6 cups chicken broth, preferably low-sodium

1¼ pounds boneless, skinless chicken breasts

1 pound fresh or frozen green beans, trimmed

6 to 8 ounces dried rice-stick noodles or vermicelli, softened in boiling water for 10 minutes and drained

1 can (13.5 ounces) light unsweetened coconut milk (about 1½ cups)

2 to 3 tablespoons fresh lemon juice

2 tablespoons soy sauce, or more to taste

¼ teaspoon freshly ground black pepper

¾ to 1 cup shredded fresh basil

1. Heat the oil in a heavy soup pot over medium heat until hot. Add the onion, ginger, curry powder, and crushed red pepper and stir-fry for 15 to 20 seconds, until fragrant. Reduce the heat to medium-low, cover, and cook for 2 to 3 minutes, until the onions are almost transparent. Add the chicken broth and bring to a boil over high heat. Reduce to a low simmer and add the chicken. Cover and poach the chicken gently for about 20 minutes, or until cooked through. Remove the chicken with a slotted spoon and let cool slightly. Cut into slices about ¼ inch thick.

2. While the chicken is cooking, bring a large pot of water to a boil. Cut the green beans on a diagonal, add to the boiling water, and cook for 5 to 6 minutes, until crisp-tender. Use a slotted

spoon to transfer the beans to a bowl of cold water, then drain. Bring the water back to a boil, add the rice noodles, and cook for 1 minute, or until tender. Drain and rinse under warm water. Drain again, then divide the noodles evenly among 6 soup bowls.

3. Reheat the soup until just under a boil. Add the coconut milk, lemon juice, soy sauce, and black pepper and bring nearly to a boil. Add the chicken and green beans, stir, and taste for seasoning, adding more soy sauce if necessary. Cook until the chicken and beans are heated through. Remove from the heat, stir in the basil, and ladle over the rice noodles.

VARIATIONS: *Add 1½ pounds butternut squash, peeled and cut into 1-inch cubes, to the soup with the chicken.*

Add 1 square firm tofu, cut into ½-inch cubes, to the soup with the chicken.

Substitute 1 pound peas, shelled edamame, or cauliflower or broccoli cut into individual florets for the green beans and cook each vegetable for 1 to 3½ minutes, until just tender.

Coconut milk is warming, counteracts the effects of summer heat, quenches thirst, and replenishes yin fluids. Recent research has shown that it contains components with antibacterial, antifungal, and antiviral properties, so it strengthens immunity and has been shown to prevent heart disease.

SOOTHING SAIGON-STYLE CHICKEN NOODLE SOUP

6 SERVINGS

Pho (pronounced "fa") is the celebrated Vietnamese rice noodle soup that many Westerners (including me) have come to know and love. It can be eaten for breakfast, lunch, or dinner. The rich broth, which is infused with cinnamon sticks, star anise, and ginger, is most commonly flavored with beef bones and meat, but the South Vietnamese like to use chicken. Making the soup can be time consuming, but by using boned chicken thighs, you cut the cooking time dramatically and still get the flavor that rivals the traditional recipe.

2 teaspoons olive or canola oil

6 to 8 slices fresh ginger about the size of a quarter, smashed with the flat side of a knife

2 whole star anise pods, smashed with the flat edge of a knife, or 1 tablespoon anise seeds

2 cinnamon sticks

4 cups chicken broth, preferably low-sodium

½ cup rice wine or sake

1½ cups water

1½ pounds boneless, skinless chicken thighs, trimmed of fat and gristle

6 ounces rice stick noodles or vermicelli, softened in boiling water for 10 minutes

5½ tablespoons fish sauce, or more to taste

3½ to 4 cups bean sprouts, rinsed and drained

½ cup shredded fresh cilantro leaves

¾ cup shredded Thai holy basil or fresh basil leaves

Lime wedges (optional)

1. Heat the oil in a heavy soup pot over medium heat and add the ginger, star anise, and cinnamon sticks. Stir-fry for 10 to 15 seconds, until fragrant. Add the chicken broth, rice wine, and water and bring to a boil. Reduce the heat to medium-low and add the chicken. Cover and cook for 25 to 30 minutes, until the chicken is cooked through. Transfer the chicken to a plate with a slotted spoon and cool slightly. Cut into 1-inch pieces. Using a fine-meshed strainer, remove the seasonings from the soup and discard. Skim the surface of the soup, removing any impurities or fat. Keep the soup warm.

(continued)

2. While the chicken is cooking, drain the rice noodles. Bring a large pot of water to a boil, add the rice noodles, and cook for 1 minute, or until tender. Drain and rinse under warm water. Drain again, then divide the noodles evenly among 6 soup bowls.

3. Add the chicken pieces, fish sauce, and bean sprouts to the soup and taste for seasoning, adding more fish sauce if necessary. Heat to just under a simmer. Add the cilantro and basil, stir, and ladle the soup over the noodles. Serve immediately with a wedge or two of fresh lime on the side if desired.

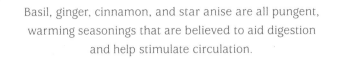

Basil, ginger, cinnamon, and star anise are all pungent, warming seasonings that are believed to aid digestion and help stimulate circulation.

GINGERY FAUX-WONTON SOUP
WITH BOW-TIE PASTA

6 TO 8 SERVINGS

When I lived in Taipei, our family Sunday lunch often consisted of a meal-in-one soup, dumplings, or a fried rice dish. My Chinese mother, sister, and I would form a production line and make trays of dumplings or wontons in record time. These days, I don't have the time (or help) to do this, so I've developed a simple method to make faux wontons using seasoned meatballs and bow-tie pasta.

MEATBALLS

- 1 pound lean ground pork
- 3 1/2 tablespoons chopped fresh ginger
- 1/4 cup chopped scallions, white parts only
- 3 tablespoons soy sauce
- 2 tablespoons rice wine or sake
- 1 egg, lightly beaten
- 1 1/2 teaspoons toasted sesame oil
- 1 1/2 tablespoons cornstarch

SOUP

- 1 bunch Swiss chard (about 1 pound)
- 1 teaspoon olive or canola oil
- 1 1/2 tablespoons chopped garlic
- 6 cups chicken broth, preferably low-sodium
- 1 1/2 cups bow-tie pasta (farfalle)
- 1 teaspoon salt or to taste
- 1/4 teaspoon freshly ground black pepper

1. To make the Meatballs: In a medium-size bowl, mix together all the ingredients, stirring vigorously with a wooden spoon to form a stiff paste. Dip a serving spoon into a cup of water to prevent it from sticking, and, using your hands and the spoon, scoop out a generous tablespoon of the mixture and roll it into a ball. Place the meatball on a sheet of wax paper and repeat to make 20 meatballs.

2. To make the Soup: Cut off the root end of the Swiss chard and discard several inches of the thick stalk end. Trim and discard any wilted leaves. Cut the remaining stalk and leaves crosswise into thin ribbons, about 1/2 inch wide, separating the stalk from the leafy sections.

3. Heat the oil in a heavy soup pot over medium-high heat until hot, about 10 seconds. Add the stalk sections of the Swiss chard and the garlic and stir-fry for 2 to 3 minutes. Add the chicken broth, partially cover, and bring to a boil. Reduce the heat to medium, add the meatballs and pasta, and cook for 10 to 12 minutes, until the pasta is almost tender. Add the green sections of the chard, partially cover, and continue cooking for 1 to 2 minutes, skimming the surface of the soup to remove any impurities. Add the salt and pepper and taste for seasoning, adjusting if necessary. Serve immediately.

CHEF CHANG'S CINNAMON BEEF NOODLES

6 SERVINGS

Along with chicken soup with ginger, this hearty and warming beef noodle stew is one of my favorite panaceas. I like to make a big pot of the soy-braised beef, freeze it in batches, then defrost and reheat, adding greens and spooning over noodles for an instant, filling lunch or dinner.

1 teaspoon olive or canola oil

RED PEPPER-CINNAMON SEASONINGS

8 cloves garlic, smashed with the flat side of a knife and peeled

6 scallions (1 bunch), ends trimmed, cut into 2-inch pieces, and smashed with the flat side of a knife

6 slices fresh ginger about the size of a quarter, smashed with the flat side of a knife

2 star anise pods, smashed with the flat side of a knife, or 1 teaspoon anise seeds

2 cinnamon sticks

1 teaspoon crushed red pepper flakes

8 1/2 cups water

5 tablespoons soy sauce

1/4 cup rice wine or sake

2 pounds beef stew meat, such as chuck or bottom round, trimmed of fat and gristle and cut into 1 1/2-inch cubes

8 ounces whole wheat spaghetti

7 to 8 ounces baby spinach, rinsed and drained

1/4 cup chopped scallion greens (optional garnish)

1. Heat the oil in a large heavy pot or casserole dish over medium-high heat until very hot. Add the Red Pepper-Cinnamon Seasonings and stir-fry until fragrant, about 15 seconds. Add the water, soy sauce, and rice wine, cover, and bring to a boil. Add the beef pieces, cover, and bring back to a boil. Partially cover, reduce the heat to low, and simmer for 1 1/2 hours, or until the beef is very tender. Skim the surface of the liquid to remove any impurities and discard. Using tongs, remove the ginger slices and the cinnamon sticks and discard.

2. While the beef is cooking, heat a large pot of water to boil. Add the whole wheat spaghetti and cook according to the package instructions until al dente. Drain in a colander and rinse under warm water. Drain again and divide evenly among 6 soup bowls.

3. Add the spinach to the soup, stir, cover, and cook for 2 to 3 minutes, until it wilts. Ladle some of the meat, spinach, and broth over the noodles, sprinkle with the chopped scallions, if using, and serve immediately.

MAIN DISH SALADS

I WAS ALWAYS partial to salads, even before I lived in Asia. But when I tasted *Peng Peng* chicken—a Sichuanese cold platter composed of layers of shredded chicken and thin ribbons of cucumber arranged on a bed of tender, sliced mung bean or vermicelli sheets and drenched in a spicy sesame paste dressing—I realized that Asian salads put to shame the bowls of iceberg lettuce, cucumber, carrots, and mushy beefsteak tomatoes that I had previously consumed. The contrasting play of textures—slippery noodles, crisp cucumbers, and tender meat bathed in the creamy dressing—awakened my palate to the sensual possibilities. As I was to learn when I started to travel around Asia, particularly in Vietnam, Thailand, Laos, and Cambodia, even Chinese salads paled in comparison to their Southeast Asian cousins.

I first tasted the classic Vietnamese salad of pork and shrimp, *Goi Tom Thit*, in a restaurant in Taipei. That was another transformative experience. Slices of cooked pork and shrimp were artistically arranged on a bed of pickled shredded carrots, celery, red onion, and cucumbers, dusted with a generous handful of chopped cilantro, mint, and chopped peanuts, and served with an exquisite sweet and sour (*Noc Cham*) dressing.

Following my Vietnamese friends' lead, I took a crispy shrimp chip, filled it with a heaping pile of the tossed salad, doused it generously with some of the vibrant sauce, and took a bite. I almost swooned. My taste buds, rather than being overwhelmed, experienced a symphony of flavors and textures.

Asian salads, or cold platters, can be deliciously unpredictable, but they often follow a pattern: Multilayered compositions of diverse ingredients selected to give a full range of textures and flavors, such as sweet, sour, spicy, and salty. Cold rice vermicelli, flour, egg, and water pasta, or cellophane noodles often serve as a textural base or staple. Vegetables such as carrots, bean sprouts, celery, various lettuces, cabbages, and cucumbers are typically used with the addition of tropical fruits such as green papaya, pineapple, pomelo (a slightly drier version of grapefruit), and lychees. Each ingredient lends its unique flavor and texture. Meats (chicken, beef, or pork) or seafood (shrimp, scallops, squid, or lobster) add substance and garnishes include tofu, shredded egg crepes, dried shrimp, chopped nuts, and fresh herbs. Fresh lemon or lime juice and rice vinegar are key elements in many of the dressings, with toasted sesame oil and soy or fish sauce rounding out the taste. A host of pungent seasonings like garlic, ginger, chili peppers, scallions, lemongrass, cilantro, basil, and mint add vibrancy and freshness. Once combined, these ingredients not only add flavor, but pull the different components together as a whole.

In many Asian countries, salads are served as appetizers, but they can easily stand on their own as entrées. In China, cold dishes like *Peng Peng* chicken and similar creations with noodles, sliced vegetables, and meats, arranged in orderly patterns, are drizzled with spicy dressings and served as a starter for a multi-course banquet. I am often content to forgo the other foods.

As the recipes in this chapter illustrate, noodle salads invite spontaneity and improvisation. I often start with a classic recipe, then revise the dish using whatever vegetables are in season, catch my eye in the supermarket, or happen to be in the refrigerator. Since I'm a huge fan of wilted salads, I toss spinach, grilled scallops, and multi-colored peppers in a warm soy dressing. These dishes are especially appropriate in the warmer weather when cooking is a chore. They can be prepared in advance and served chilled or at room temperature.

Asian salads are ideal for busy cooks who have limited time. Supermarkets now offer an enticing array of sliced and shredded vegetables, shortening the preparation time of many salads. And they often cost no more than the unprepared foods. Dressings can be made in large quantities so you can have them on hand in the refrigerator. Main dish salads are not only irresistible, but with each bite, you're giving your body a generous dose of good health.

CRISP VEGETABLES AND TOFU IN A SPICY SATE DRESSING

4 TO 6 SERVINGS

This salad takes its inspiration from *Gado Gado,* a traditional Indonesian salad made with string beans, carrots, potatoes, and eggs. The peanut-coconut dressing is addictive and can also be served with grilled meat or seafood. Make big batches to keep in the refrigerator so you can instantly whip up spontaneous and imaginative creations of leftovers and fresh vegetables over noodles.

1 square (1 pound) extra-firm tofu

2 English seedless cucumbers, rinsed and drained

1 medium red bell pepper, cored, seeded, rinsed, and drained

8 ounces whole wheat spaghetti

2 cups shredded or grated carrots

2 cups bean sprouts, rinsed lightly and drained

3 tablespoons olive or canola oil

SATE DRESSING

$^3/_4$ cup smooth peanut butter

1 can (15 ounces) or $1^1/_2$ cups light coconut milk

$3^1/_2$ tablespoons soy sauce, or to taste

3 tablespoons freshly squeezed lime juice

$1^1/_2$ tablespoons firmly packed light brown sugar

1 teaspoon crushed red pepper flakes, or to taste

1. Cut the tofu horizontally in half and wrap in paper towels. Put a heavy weight, such as a pot, on top, and drain, changing the towels once, while preparing the other ingredients.

2. Cut the cucumbers lengthwise in half and scoop out any seeds with a spoon. Grate or shred the cucumbers, using a hand grater or a food processor fitted with a shredding disc. Using your hands, squeeze out any excess water. Cut the bell peppers into $^1/_4$-inch-thick slices.

3. Bring 3 quarts of water to a boil in a large pot. Add the whole wheat noodles and cook for a little less time than directed on the package instructions, until al dente. Drain in a colander and rinse thoroughly under warm water. Drain the noodles again and arrange in a large deep serving dish. Arrange the cucumbers, shredded carrots, and bean sprouts in separate concentric circles on top, leaving room in the center for the tofu.

(continued)

4. Heat the oil in a large skillet over medium-high until hot, about 20 seconds. Fry the tofu halves on both sides until golden brown, about 5 minutes. Drain on paper towels. Using a sharp or serrated knife, cut into slices ¼ inch thick. Arrange over the bean sprouts and sprinkle the red pepper slices on top.

5. To make the Sate Dressing: Place all the ingredients in the bowl of a food processor, or in a blender fitted with a steel blade, and mix until smooth. Drizzle half of the sauce over the salad. Pour the other half into a bowl and serve on the side. Alternatively, you may heat the sate slightly in a saucepan and serve warm on top of the room temperature vegetables and noodles.

Peanuts, a member of the legume family, are a good source of monounsaturated fat and have been shown to prevent cardiovascular disease. Chinese doctors credit them with lubricating the intestines and settling the stomach.

MULTI-COLORED TOFU SALAD
WITH MISO DRESSING

6 TO 8 SERVINGS

I've always loved the miso dressing served in Japanese restaurants, so I was determined to duplicate it in this salad. The salty-sweet flavor of *miso shiro* is a wonderful complement to the nutty soba noodles and fresh vegetables.

1 square (about 14 ounces) soft or firm tofu

1 bunch asparagus (about 1¼ pounds), woody ends snapped

8 ounces soba noodles

1 teaspoon toasted sesame oil for seasoning the noodles

MISO DRESSING

1 cup sweet white miso paste (*miso shiro*)

½ cup plus 2 tablespoons water

6 tablespoons rice vinegar

2 tablespoons mirin or 1½ tablespoons rice wine mixed with 1½ tablespoons sugar

1⅓ tablespoons low-sodium soy sauce

1 teaspoon toasted sesame oil

2 cups shredded carrots (1 6-ounce package)

1 medium red bell pepper, cored, seeded, and cut into thin julienne strips (optional)

½ bunch scallions, green parts only, minced (about 1 cup)

1. Cut the tofu horizontally in half and wrap in paper towels. Put a heavy weight such as a pot on top, and drain, changing the towels once, for about 10 minutes. Cut the pressed tofu into matchstick-size shreds.

2. Cut the asparagus into 2½-inch lengths. Bring 3 quarts of water to a boil in a large pot. Add the asparagus and cook until crisp-tender, about 5 minutes. Remove with a slotted spoon, drain thoroughly, and pat dry with paper towels. Reheat the water until boiling, add the soba noodles, and cook for 3½ to 4 minutes, until al dente or tender to the bite. Drain and rinse thoroughly and toss with the toasted sesame oil.

3. To make the Miso Dressing, put the miso paste in a medium-size mixing bowl. Slowly add the water, stirring to make a smooth paste. Stir in the remaining dressing ingredients in the listed order and pour into a small bowl.

4. Arrange the soba noodles in a large bowl. Arrange the carrots, asparagus, and tofu in separate concentric circles on the noodles. Sprinkle the top with the red bell pepper, if using, and minced scallions. Drizzle a little of the Miso Dressing on top and serve the rest on the side. If desired, chill before serving.

WARM ROASTED VEGETABLE–QUINOA SALAD

6 SERVINGS

Roasting vegetables is so easy, and you can vary the recipe depending on what's in season. I especially like to serve roasted veggies with a nutty grain like quinoa as a meal by itself, or as a side to grilled, roasted, or pan-seared meat or seafood.

2 medium fennel bulbs (about 1½ pounds), rinsed, drained, and stems cut off and discarded

2 medium red onions, peeled

1 pound baby carrots, rinsed and drained

1 package (8 ounces) teriyaki, Thai, or lemon pepper–flavored baked tofu (optional)

FLAVORINGS (combine in a small bowl)

½ cup balsamic vinegar

⅓ cup fruity extra-virgin olive oil

3 tablespoons minced fresh ginger

1 cup quinoa

1½ teaspoons virgin olive oil

1¼ cups water

DRESSING (combine in a small bowl and stir until the sugar dissolves)

3 tablespoons soy sauce

6 tablespoons water

5 tablespoons chopped fresh parsley

1 tablespoon minced garlic

2 teaspoons sugar

1. Preheat the oven to 425°F. Trim the stem end of the fennel bulbs, leaving ⅛ inch of the root base, and cut each fennel bulb in half. With the cut edge down, cut each half into thin slices about ¼ inch thick. Place in a large mixing bowl.

2. Cut the red onions in half, then cut each half into ¼-inch-thick slices. Put in the bowl and add the carrots. If using baked tofu, cut into ¼-inch-thick slices 1½ inches long and add to the vegetables.

3. Pour the Flavorings over the vegetables and toss lightly to coat. Transfer the vegetables to a large roasting pan or a cookie sheet and roast for about 40 minutes. Flip the vegetables over and continue baking for another 20 minutes, or until the vegetables are tender and golden brown at the edges.

4. Rinse the quinoa in a bowl, using your hands as a rake, and drain in a sieve. Heat the oil in a saucepan with a lid over medium-high until hot, about 20 seconds. Add the quinoa and toast, stirring with a wooden spoon, until golden brown, 4 to 5 minutes. Add the water and bring to a boil. Reduce the heat to low, cover, and cook for 15 minutes, until the liquid is absorbed and the quinoa is tender. Remove from the heat, uncover, and fluff with a fork.

5. Spoon the quinoa into the bottom of a large serving bowl. Spoon the roasted vegetables over the quinoa. Prepare then pour the Dressing over all. Toss lightly and serve warm or at room temperature.

VARIATION: *Substitute eggplant, sweet potatoes, zucchini, asparagus, or other vegetables for the fennel, and roast until tender.*

Quinoa is a nutty grain and a great source of protein
and fiber. It is also gluten-free, easy to digest,
and high in magnesium and iron.

BROWN RICE SALAD
WITH SHRIMP AND AVOCADO

4 TO 6 SERVINGS

Once cooked, brown rice has a firm texture that is particularly good in rice salads and fried rice dishes. I like to make a big batch and freeze 2-cup portions in freezer bags. You can pull them from the freezer, microwave or steam for several minutes or longer, and you have instant cooked rice.

1 pound raw medium shrimp, peeled, deveined, rinsed, and drained

4 slices fresh ginger about the size of a quarter, smashed lightly with the flat side of a knife

2 tablespoons rice wine or sake

2 ripe avocados

Juice of 1 lemon

4 cups cooked brown rice (see page 113) at room temperature

DRESSING (combine in a small bowl)

$\frac{1}{3}$ cup soy sauce

3 to 4 tablespoons rice vinegar

1$\frac{1}{2}$ tablespoons rice wine or sake

1$\frac{1}{2}$ tablespoons toasted sesame oil

1$\frac{1}{2}$ tablespoons sugar

1 teaspoon salt

1 cup chopped fresh flat-leaf parsley

$\frac{1}{2}$ cup chopped fresh cilantro, leaves only

1. Using a sharp knife, cut the shrimp in half lengthwise along the back. Place in a bowl, add the smashed ginger and rice wine, and toss lightly.

2. Bring 2 quarts water to a boil in a large pot. Add the shrimp and marinade and cook for 2$\frac{1}{2}$ to 3 minutes, until cooked through. Drain in a colander, discard the ginger slices, and let the shrimp cool.

3. Cut the avocados in half, remove the pits, and cut the flesh into $\frac{1}{2}$-inch dice. In a large mixing or serving bowl, lightly toss the avocado with half the lemon juice. Add the cooked shrimp and rice. Add the remaining lemon juice and toss. Prepare and add the Dressing, parsley, and cilantro; toss lightly. Taste for seasoning, adding more salt if necessary. Serve at room temperature or chilled.

VARIATION: *Replace the chopped cilantro with fresh dill, tarragon, or another herb of your choice.*

TANDOORI SHRIMP WITH FENNEL
IN ORANGE-GINGER DRESSING

6 SERVINGS

Thin slices of fresh, licorice-like fennel are a lovely complement to spicy shrimp with a fresh orange-ginger dressing. If given a choice in the store, select bluish-tinged shrimp, rather than pink, since they have a crunchier texture once cooked. Serve this dish with whole grain bread, couscous, or another grain for a light yet filling meal.

1½ pounds raw medium shrimp, peeled, deveined, rinsed, and drained

TANDOORI MARINADE (combine in a medium bowl)

2 tablespoons rice wine or sake

1 tablespoon chopped garlic

1½ teaspoons ground cumin

1½ teaspoons ground coriander

2 fennel bulbs (1½ pounds)

ORANGE DRESSING (whisk together in a large bowl)

2 teaspoons chopped or grated orange zest from 1 orange

½ cup fresh orange juice

⅓ cup fruity extra-virgin olive oil

2½ tablespoons Japanese rice vinegar, or to taste

2 tablespoons minced fresh ginger

1½ teaspoons sugar

1¼ teaspoons salt

¼ teaspoon freshly ground black pepper

2 tablespoons olive or canola oil for frying shrimp

2 cups coarsely chopped fresh flat-leaf parsley

1. Using a sharp knife, score the shrimp lengthwise along the back to butterfly. Add to the bowl with the Tandoori Marinade, toss lightly, and let sit for 15 minutes.

2. Trim the fennel stalks and root base, reserving the fronds or leaves. Hold the fennel bulb securely and cut lengthwise in half, then cut into thin slices. Tear the fennel fronds into small pieces and set aside. Add the fennel slices to the Orange Dressing in the large bowl and mix together to coat. Cover and let sit or refrigerate to chill slightly.

3. Heat the oil in a nonstick skillet over medium-high heat until very hot, about 20 seconds. Add the shrimp and stir-fry for about 3 minutes, until opaque and cooked. Remove and drain.

4. Reserve some of the parsley and fennel fronds for garnish. Add the shrimp and the remaining chopped parsley and fennel fronds to the sliced fennel and dressing. Toss lightly to coat. Taste for seasoning, adding more salt and pepper if necessary. Sprinkle the reserved parsley and fennel fronds on top. Serve immediately or chill and serve.

VARIATION: *Substitute scallops, sliced chicken, or pork for the shrimp, increasing the cooking time slightly for the meat if necessary.*

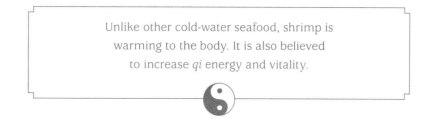

Unlike other cold-water seafood, shrimp is warming to the body. It is also believed to increase *qi* energy and vitality.

WILTED SPINACH AND SCALLOP SALAD WITH TOASTED SESAME SEEDS

4 SERVINGS

Although this is not classic Chinese fare, my master chef teachers would approve of this warm salad with its combination of baby spinach, sautéed scallops, and tart dressing topped with toasted sesame seeds. You may substitute shrimp, crab, or chicken for the scallops.

1 pound large sea scallops, muscles removed
    and rinsed and drained

2 tablespoons rice wine or sake

1 teaspoon minced fresh ginger

2 ½ tablespoons olive or canola oil

1 pound baby spinach, rinsed and drained

2 roasted red peppers, blotted dry
    (or use roasted peppers from a jar),
    cut into ¼-inch dice

DRESSING (combine in a small bowl)

½ cup light soy sauce

5 tablespoons clear rice vinegar

2 ½ tablespoons sugar

3 tablespoons sesame seeds, toasted in a
    nonstick pan until golden brown (optional)

1. Holding a knife horizontal to the cutting board, slice the scallops horizontally in half. Place in a bowl, add the rice wine and ginger, and toss lightly. Let sit briefly.

2. Heat a large skillet or wok over high heat. Add 1½ tablespoons of the oil and heat until very hot, but not smoking. Drain the scallops and add to the pan. (If too many, fry in two batches.) Pan-fry over high heat for about 3 minutes on each side, until the scallops are golden and cooked through. Remove with a large slotted spoon or strainer.

3. Place the spinach in a salad or deep serving bowl. Arrange the cooked scallops over the spinach.

4. Wipe the pan, add the remaining 1 tablespoon oil, and heat until hot. Add the red peppers and stir-fry lightly over high heat, about 30 seconds. Add the Dressing and stir-fry until just under a boil. Pour the hot dressing over the spinach and scallops and sprinkle the top with the toasted sesame seeds, if using. Toss lightly and serve immediately.

> Spinach is not only rich in iron and chlorophyll, which helps to fortify blood, but also abundant in vitamin A. According to Chinese doctors, it helps to hydrate the body and quenches thirst.

SEARED GINGER-BALSAMIC SALMON
WITH HOT AND SOUR SLAW

4 SERVINGS

Due in large part to its health-giving omega-3 oils, salmon has become one of the most popular types of fish consumed in the United States. I prefer to buy wild salmon for its flavor. The seared salmon and easy slaw are excellent served hot, room temperature, or cold.

4 pieces (6 ounces each) center-cut salmon fillets with skin, patted dry

1 teaspoon salt

½ teaspoon freshly ground black pepper

4 teaspoons olive or canola oil

1 teaspoon toasted sesame oil

2 tablespoons chopped fresh ginger

1 teaspoon crushed red pepper flakes

1 medium red pepper, cored, seeded, and cut into dice

1 bag (9 ounces) shredded broccoli slaw (3½ cups)

2 tablespoons rice wine or sake

HOT AND SOUR DRESSING (combine in a small bowl)

¼ cup soy sauce

3 tablespoons sugar

2 tablespoons Chinese black vinegar or Worcestershire sauce

¼ teaspoon salt

1 cup water

¼ cup balsamic vinegar

2 tablespoons fresh lemon juice

2 tablespoons minced fresh ginger

1½ tablespoons firmly packed light brown sugar

1. Season the salmon fillets with the salt and pepper.

2. In a wok or heavy skillet, heat 2 teaspoons of the olive or canola oil and the sesame oil over high heat until hot, but not smoking. Add the ginger and red pepper flakes and stir-fry until fragrant, about 10 seconds. Add the diced red pepper and toss lightly over high heat. Add the broccoli slaw, toss lightly, and pour in the rice wine. Stir and cover. Cook over medium-high heat for a minute or two. Uncover and add the Hot and Sour Dressing. Toss lightly for a minute and remove to a serving bowl.

3. Heat the remaining 2 teaspoons oil in a 12-inch nonstick skillet over medium-high heat until very hot, about 10 seconds. Arrange the salmon fillets in the pan, skin side up. Partially cover and sear until well browned, 5 to 6 minutes. Turn the fish over and continue cooking for 5 to 6 minutes, until the fish flakes in the middle when prodded with a knife.

(continued)

4. Using a slotted spoon or a spatula, portion the slaw on 4 individual serving plates (or keep in the serving bowl). Place the cooked salmon fillets on top.

5. Drain off any oil and reheat the pan with the water, balsamic vinegar, lemon juice, ginger, and brown sugar, stirring to combine. Simmer over medium-heat high heat for 1½ to 2 minutes, until thickened and reduced to ⅓ cup. Carefully pour the glaze over the salmon. Serve with rice or another whole grain.

> Broccoli is a member of the cruciferous family, which means it contains phytonutrients that lower the risk of cancer. In addition, broccoli is an excellent source of vitamins A and C and calcium and fiber.

CURRY-COCONUT CHICKEN AND MANGO SALAD

6 SERVINGS

Part salad, part noodle entrée, this unusual dish hits all the flavor sweet spots: savory, sweet, sour, and spicy. It's delectable year-round, but especially good in warm weather.

6 ounces thin rice stick or vermicelli noodles, covered in boiling water for 10 minutes

12 ounces frozen shelled edamame, defrosted (about 2½ cups)

2 firm-ripe mangoes (about 1½ pounds), pitted, peeled, and cut into 1-inch squares

1½ pounds cooked boneless, skinless chicken breasts, cut into thin julienne strips

½ cup fresh cilantro or basil leaves, cut into thin shreds or torn into small pieces

1 teaspoon olive or canola oil

1 teaspoon crushed red pepper flakes (optional)

2 teaspoons Madras curry powder

1 can (15 ounces) or 1½ cups light unsweetened coconut milk

3 tablespoons fish sauce, or to taste

3 tablespoons fresh lime juice

1½ tablespoons sugar

1. Bring 3 quarts water to a boil in a large pot. Drain the soaked rice noodles and add to the pot, swirling them around in the water for a minute or so, then drain in a colander. Refresh under cold running water and drain.

2. Arrange the cooked noodles in a large, fairly deep serving bowl. Mix the edamame with the mango pieces and sprinkle on top, leaving a slight well in the center. Arrange the chicken pieces in the center and sprinkle the chopped cilantro or basil on top.

3. Heat the oil in a skillet over medium heat until hot, about 10 seconds. Add the red pepper flakes, if using, and the curry powder and stir-fry until fragrant, about 15 seconds. Add the coconut milk, fish sauce, lime juice, and sugar and bring to a boil, stirring to dissolve the sugar. Pour some of the dressing on top of the salad and serve the remainder on the side in a bowl or saucer, allowing diners to help themselves. Serve warm or at room temperature.

VARIATION: *Substitute cooked shrimp, scallops, firm-fleshed fish fillets, pork, or turkey for the chicken.*

Mangoes are not only an excellent source of vitamins A and C, but Chinese doctors believe they also regenerate body fluids and aid digestion.

EASY BASIL CHICKEN SALAD WITH SOBA

6 SERVINGS

Soba noodles are a versatile staple with a deliciously nutty flavor that works well in hot soups, stir-fries, and cold appetizers. Usually, they are served cold with a smoky soy *dashi* broth and wasabi. I like to toss them with a spicy, fresh basil pesto and use it as a base for a shredded chicken and snow pea salad, topped with a piquant dressing. It's an easy, meal-in-one dish and one of my family's and friends' favorites.

¾ pound snow or snap peas, ends snapped and veiny strings removed

12 ounces soba noodles

SPICY PESTO

6 cloves garlic, smashed and peeled

4 scallions, white parts only, cut into 1-inch pieces (reserve the greens for the garnish)

1 teaspoon crushed red pepper flakes

2 cups fresh basil leaves, rinsed, drained, and patted dry

2 tablespoons toasted sesame oil

1 tablespoon olive or canola oil

2 tablespoons fresh lemon juice

1 tablespoon soy sauce

1 pound cooked boneless, skinless chicken breasts, cut into thin julienne strips

Reserved scallion greens, cut into ¼-inch sections

DRESSING (combine in a small bowl until the sugar dissolves)

½ cup light soy sauce, or to taste

6 tablespoons Japanese clear rice vinegar

2 tablespoons mirin, or rice wine or sake, mixed with 1 tablespoon sugar

1½ tablespoons sugar

1. Bring 3 quarts of water to a boil in a large pot. Add the snow peas and cook for 30 seconds. Remove with a large slotted spoon and drain in a strainer or colander under cold running water. Bring the water to a boil again and add the soba noodles. Once the water boils again, cook for 3½ minutes, or until al dente. Drain in a colander and rinse the noodles under warm running water. Drain again.

(continued)

2. To make the Spicy Pesto: Drop the garlic, scallion whites, and red pepper flakes down the feed tube of a food processor while the motor is running and chop finely. Open up the bowl and add the basil leaves. Pulse, turning the machine on and off, then slowly pour the sesame and olive oil down the feed tube and chop the mixture to a fine paste. Add the lemon juice and soy sauce and continue blending until the mixture is a fairly smooth paste.

3. In a large mixing bowl, toss the cooked soba noodles with the pesto mixture. Arrange in a large shallow bowl or platter. Sprinkle the snap peas evenly over the noodles, followed by the julienned chicken, and finishing with the scallion greens. Serve the Dressing on the side in a sauce bowl, or drizzle over the salad. Serve at room temperature or chilled.

VARIATION: *Substitute cooked shrimp, pork, or flavored tofu for the chicken. You can also replace the snow or snap peas with 2½ cups shredded carrots, bean sprouts, or other sliced vegetables.*

CHICKEN NOODLE SALAD
WITH SPICY TAHINI DRESSING

6 SERVINGS

Sichuanese chefs make a spicy toasted sesame dressing for the popular classic, *Dan Dan* noodles. Drawing inspiration from that dish, I've created a similar sauce using untoasted tahini paste, which is sold in every supermarket. The flavor is lighter, but no less appealing. Make a big batch and refrigerate so you can spontaneously prepare a salad for a quick and healthy meal.

$3\frac{3}{4}$ to 4 ounces cellophane noodles, covered in boiling water for 10 minutes

2 English seedless cucumbers, cut in half lengthwise

2 cups shredded or grated carrots

2 cups bean sprouts, rinsed and drained

1 pound cooked boneless, skinless chicken breasts, cut into thin julienne strips

3 scallions, green parts only, cut into $\frac{1}{2}$-inch lengths

SPICY TAHINI DRESSING

1 cup sesame tahini paste

10 tablespoons water

$\frac{1}{4}$ cup toasted sesame oil

$\frac{1}{4}$ cup soy sauce

3 tablespoons rice wine or sake

$\frac{1}{4}$ cup sugar

$\frac{1}{4}$ cup minced fresh ginger

3 tablespoons minced garlic

$1\frac{1}{2}$ teaspoons hot chili paste, or to taste

1. Bring 3 quarts of water to a boil in a large pot. Drain the soaked cellophane noodles and add to the pot. Cook for about 1 minute, until tender. Drain in a colander and rinse under cold running water. Drain thoroughly.

2. Scoop out any seeds from the cucumber with a spoon, then grate or shred the cucumber using the shredding blade of a food processor. Using your hands, squeeze out the liquid.

3. Arrange the cellophane noodles in a large serving bowl. Arrange the carrots, cucumbers, and bean sprouts in concentric circles on top of the noodles, leaving a space in the middle. Arrange the chicken in the center. Sprinkle the scallion greens on top.

(continued)

4. To make the Spicy Tahini Dressing: Combine all the ingredients in a blender or the bowl of a food processor fitted with a steel blade and blend thoroughly. Taste for seasoning, adjusting if necessary. Drizzle a little of the dressing on top of the salad and serve the remainder in a bowl on the side. Serve the salad at room temperature or chilled.

VARIATION: *Substitute pork, seafood, or tofu for the chicken and top the noodles with different vegetables, including cooked green beans, sliced peppers, snow or snap peas, or shredded lettuce.*

While black sesame seeds, which are sold in Asian markets, are considered to be more beneficial than tan sesame seeds, the two share many of the same properties, including their ability to strengthen the liver and kidneys and lubricate the intestines.

VIETNAMESE GRILLED PORK
WITH BASIL AND FRESH LIME DRESSING

6 SERVINGS

This is my streamlined version of a classic Vietnamese salad, *Goi Thom Thit*. Usually shrimp is added, and it is generally served with fried shrimp chips. Instead, I like to serve it over tender rice sticks that round out the dish and soak up the piquant dressing.

1½ pounds boneless pork tenderloin, trimmed of fat and gristle

MARINADE (combine in a small bowl)

¼ cup soy sauce

2 tablespoons rice wine or sake

1½ tablespoons chopped garlic

6 ounces thin rice stick or vermicelli noodles, softened in boiling water for 10 minutes and drained

Olive oil spray or 1½ tablespoons canola oil

3 cups Boston or other lettuce leaves, cut into thin shreds

2 cups shredded or grated carrots

2 cups bean sprouts, rinsed and drained

½ cup fresh basil leaves, cut into shreds or ripped into small pieces

¼ cup coarsely chopped dry-roasted peanuts (optional)

VIETNAMESE DRESSING (combine in a small bowl and stir until the sugar dissolves)

Juice of 4 to 5 limes or 2½ lemons (about ⅔ cup)

⅓ cup fish sauce, or more to taste

⅓ cup sugar

1½ tablespoons minced garlic

1 teaspoon crushed red pepper flakes, or to taste

1. Place the pork in a shallow dish, add the Marinade, and rub to coat. Cover with plastic wrap and let stand while mixing the dressing and preparing the other ingredients.

2. Bring 3 quarts water to a boil in a large pot. Add the rice noodles, swishing them around in the water for a minute or so, then drain in a colander. Refresh under cold running water and drain thoroughly.

(continued)

3. Prepare a medium-hot fire for grilling and spray or brush the grill rack with the oil, or heat a skillet and heat the oil in the pan until hot, about 15 seconds. Grill or pan-sear the pork (covered) for 9 to 10 minutes on each side, or until the internal temperature registers 145°F to 150°F. Transfer to a cutting board and let rest for 5 minutes. Cut into thin slices about $\frac{1}{4}$ inch thick.

4. Place the noodles in the bottom of a large serving bowl or platter and arrange the lettuce, carrots, and bean sprouts in separate concentric circles on top. Sprinkle the pork evenly over the vegetables and top with the shredded basil and chopped peanuts, if using. Pour some of the Vietnamese Dressing over the top and serve the remainder in a bowl or saucer on the side. Serve at room temperature or chilled.

VARIATION: *Substitute grilled or pan-seared chicken, seafood, or beef for the pork, and vary the vegetables depending on what is in season.*

SAUCY GARLIC-ROASTED PORK
WITH BROCCOLI SLAW

4 TO 6 SERVINGS

The combination of roasted meat and hot and sour slaw is popular all over the world, and China is no exception. Using shredded broccoli slaw cuts preparation time and, unlike cabbage, broccoli remains crisp-tender even after stir-frying. To remove the raw flavor, briefly blanch the broccoli slaw for 30 seconds in boiling water, refresh in cold water, and drain.

1¼ pounds pork tenderloin, trimmed of fat and gristle

MARINADE/SAUCE (combine in a small bowl)

   ¾ cup hoisin sauce

   5 tablespoons soy sauce

   2 tablespoons rice wine or sake

   2 tablespoons chopped garlic

   2 tablespoons chopped fresh ginger

   ½ cup water

½ pound angel hair pasta, whole wheat spaghetti, or vermicelli noodles

1 teaspoon toasted sesame oil

1 bag (9 ounces) shredded broccoli slaw (3½ cups)

1½ cups grated or shredded carrots

1. Preheat the oven to 375°F. Line a roasting pan with aluminum foil.

2. Put the trimmed pork in a bowl. Spoon one-third of the Marinade over the pork and spread to cover. Pour the remaining marinade into a small saucepan and set aside. Place the pork and its marinade in the prepared pan and roast, periodically spooning the marinade on top, for 45 to 50 minutes, until the internal temperature reaches 150°F. Remove and let cool slightly Cut across the grain into thin slices.

3. Bring 3 quarts of water to a boil in a large pot. Add the noodles and cook a bit less than the package instructions indicate, until al dente. Drain in a colander and rinse under cold running water. Drain again and, using kitchen shears, cut into 4- to 6-inch lengths. Toss the noodles with the toasted sesame oil.

(continued)

4. Bring the remaining marinade mixture to a boil, stirring occasionally. Keep warm in the saucepan.

5. Arrange the noodles in a serving bowl. Sprinkle the broccoli slaw and carrots in separate concentric circles on top, reserving the center for the pork slices. Drizzle some of the warm sauce on top of the vegetables and pour the rest in a saucer to serve on the side. Arrange the pork slices over the shredded vegetables and serve warm, at room temperature, or chilled.

VARIATION: *Substitute chicken or very firm tofu for the pork and bake for about 30 minutes, or until completely cooked. Use shredded or grated cucumber, cabbage, peppers, blanched snow or snap peas, or other vegetables in place of the broccoli slaw and carrots.*

WARM TERIYAKI PEPPER-STEAK SALAD

6 SERVINGS

I like to make a big batch of the teriyaki sauce and keep it in my fridge. It is an ideal sauce for grilling beef, pork, chicken, tofu, all types of seafood, and vegetables. It will keep for weeks in a sealed container.

GARLIC TERIYAKI SAUCE

$2/3$ cup water

$1/3$ cup soy sauce

$1/3$ cup rice wine

5 tablespoons sugar

2 tablespoons minced garlic

2 teaspoons cornstarch

$1\frac{1}{2}$ pounds top sirloin steak, trimmed of fat and gristle

$1/2$ pound snow or snap peas, ends snapped and strings removed

8 ounces soba noodles

$1\frac{1}{2}$ teaspoons toasted sesame oil

2 roasted red peppers

2 tablespoons olive or canola oil or spray for oiling the grill

1. To make the Garlic Teriyaki Sauce: Mix all the ingredients in a saucepan over medium heat and heat until the mixture boils and thickens. Remove from the heat. Pour one-third into a shallow dish large enough to hold the meat, and let cool. Leave the remaining sauce in the pan and keep warm.

2. Put the steak in the shallow dish and rub the surface with the marinade. Cover and let marinate at room temperature for 15 to 20 minutes. Cut the snow peas lengthwise in half.

3. Bring 3 quarts of water to a boil in a large pot. Add the snow or snap peas and blanch for about 30 seconds. Remove with a handled strainer and refresh in a colander under cold running water. Drain thoroughly. Bring the water back to a boil, add the soba noodles and stir to separate. Cook for $3\frac{1}{2}$ minutes, or until al dente. Drain, rinse under warm running water, and drain thoroughly. Mix the noodles with the sesame oil and place in a large bowl. Cut the peppers into thin julienne strips and mix with the snow or snap peas. Sprinkle over the noodles.

4. Prepare a medium-hot fire for grilling or preheat a gas grill. Brush or spray the grill rack with oil. Grill the beef for 6 to 8 minutes on each side for medium-rare. Remove to a cutting board and let sit for 5 minutes.

5. Cut the meat across the grain into slices about ¼ inch thick. Sprinkle over the vegetables and drizzle the remaining warm garlic teriyaki sauce over all. Serve warm or at room temperature.

VARIATION: *Substitute chicken breasts, turkey tenderloin, scallops, shrimp, or firm-fleshed fish fillets for the beef and grill until completely cooked. Replace the snow peas with cooked broccoli, broccolini, broccoli rabe, bok choy or baby bok choy, kale, spinach, or other vegetables.*

Peppers are excellent sources of vitamins A and C,
as well as a powerful source of antioxidants. Red peppers
in particular contain lycopene, a phytonutrient
believed to prevent prostate cancer as well as cancers
of the cervix, bladder, and pancreas.

CHAPTER 3

❧

STIR-FRY SUPPERS

STIR-FRY SUPPERS

ANY COOK, EVEN a novice, can master stir-frying. It's less magic than method. The secret lies in being organized and knowing a few basics. This age-old cooking method is especially appropriate for a weeknight dinner when the food has to be quick, easy, and delicious. And did I mention that it's healthy?

Stir-frying is one of the simplest cooking methods of Asian cooks, and it invites improvisation. Select ingredients with regard for contrasting and complementary flavors, colors, and textures. Stir-fried dishes are usually made up of three main components: *protein*, *vegetables*, and *sauce*. The protein can be mixed and matched with all kinds of vegetables, depending on the season and whatever is readily available.

Proteins include meats, seafood, or tofu or tofu products. Choose the leanest, most tender cuts of meats:

- For chicken, use boneless chicken breasts or thighs.

- For pork, choose the tenderloin or center-cut fillet.

- For beef, use top round steak, flank steak, or London broil.

- For seafood, use shrimp, scallops, squid, or firm, "meaty" fish fillets such as striped bass, tilapia, or mahimahi.

Vegetables fall into two groups based on the amount of time they need to cook:

- Firm vegetables include asparagus, broccoli, broccolini, broccoli rabe, bell peppers, cauliflower, bok choy, carrots, celery, mushrooms, onions, leeks, squash (summer and winter), green beans, eggplant, edamame, and peas.

- Leafy vegetables include spinach, cabbage (Chinese and Western), watercress, kale, Swiss chard, and other greens. Bean sprouts belong in this group because they cook quickly.

Don't be afraid to improvise, but remember that organization is the key to successful stir-frying. For optimum flavor, the dish should be served as soon as it comes out of the pan. As Chinese chefs often told me, the guests can wait for the food, but the food should never wait for the guests.

STIR-FRY IN FOUR EASY STEPS

ONE: CUT INGREDIENTS AND MARINATE (WHEN NECESSARY)

Uniformity in type and size is important so that the food will cook evenly. Some meats and seafood should be marinated to add flavor and tenderize.

TWO: PREPARE SEASONINGS AND MIX SAUCE

Garlic, ginger, scallions, leeks, hot pepper, and sweet peppers are often called for in stir-fry recipes. Seasonings and sauces can be combined in a bowl. Mix an additional 1 teaspoon of cornstarch with 2 tablespoons of water in another bowl, to add if necessary. Place all the ingredients near the stove.

THREE: PRECOOK PROTEIN AND VEGETABLE (WHEN NECESSARY)

Traditionally, meat or seafood is shallow-fried in a little oil at a high temperature roughly 400°F, until cooked. Cook over high heat until the food turns opaque and is evenly cooked. Remove and drain in a colander.

Alternatively, grilling, steaming, or roasting are also excellent methods.

Firm vegetables that require precooking (such as broccoli, bok choy, green beans, etc.) can be parboiled, steamed, or roasted until "crisp-tender." When parboiling, refresh the vegetables in cold water after cooking to prevent overcooking and to keep the colors bright.

FOUR: STIR-FRY

The final step of stir-frying is *fast*. Heat the pan before adding the oil. This will accelerate the stir-fry process. Then heat the oil until hot before adding the seasonings. Cook the seasonings until fragrant. All the ingredients are then added and tossed together until the sauce thickens. Heat should be at the highest possible level, giving the dish a unique, "pan-seared" flavor. Serve immediately

GINGERY SHRIMP WITH ASPARAGUS AND EDAMAME

6 SERVINGS

The beauty of many stir-fried dishes is their simplicity, and this one is no exception. Since the sauce is light and subtle, make certain to use top-quality ingredients. I recommend using blue shrimp, which has a slightly crisper consistency once cooked than pink shrimp.

1 pound raw medium shrimp, peeled, deveined, rinsed, and drained

GINGER MARINADE (combine in a small bowl)

3 tablespoons rice wine or sake

1½ tablespoons minced fresh ginger

½ teaspoon toasted sesame oil

1 pound fresh asparagus

3 scallions, ends trimmed and discarded

2 tablespoons olive or canola oil

SAUCE (combine in a small bowl)

½ cup chicken broth, preferably low-sodium

1 tablespoon rice wine or sake

1 tablespoon soy sauce

1 teaspoon sugar

1 teaspoon toasted sesame oil

½ teaspoon salt

1¼ teaspoons cornstarch

½ pound frozen shelled edamame, defrosted to room temperature

1. Using a sharp knife, score the shrimp lengthwise along the back to butterfly. Place in a bowl, add the Ginger Marinade, toss lightly, and let sit while preparing the other ingredients.

2. Snap the woody ends off the asparagus and cut into 1-inch lengths. Rinse and drain thoroughly. Mince the white parts of the scallions and cut the green parts into ½-inch lengths.

3. Heat a heavy skillet or wok over high heat until hot. Add 1 tablespoon of the oil and heat for about 20 seconds. Add the shrimp and stir-fry until cooked through, about 2½ minutes. Remove the shrimp and drain.

4. Wipe the pan and reheat with the remaining 1 tablespoon oil until hot. Add the minced scallion whites and stir-fry until fragrant, about 10 seconds. Add the asparagus and ¼ cup water. Partially cover and cook over medium heat for 4 to 5 minutes, or until the asparagus is tender.

(continued)

Uncover, drain out any water, and add the Sauce, edamame, and scallion greens. Cook over high heat, stirring to prevent any lumps. Once the sauce thickens, return the shrimp and toss lightly to coat. Scoop onto a serving platter or into a bowl. Serve with steamed rice.

VARIATIONS: *Substitute chicken, scallops, or firm-fleshed fish fillets for the shrimp, increasing the cooking time until the food is cooked.*

Vary the vegetables, using bite-size pieces of bok choy, Swiss chard, broccoli, carrots, or green beans. Decrease the cooking time and cook only until the vegetables are crisp-tender.

Since asparagus contain the diuretic asparagine, Chinese doctors recommend eating it for many urinary problems. Asparagus is also believed to tone the kidneys and moisten the lungs.

SINGAPORE RICE NOODLES

6 TO 8 SERVINGS

The food of Singapore is a melting pot of diverse influences from China, Malaysia, India, and Portugal. These noodles are a fine example of this hybrid style. Pungent curry powder and ginger flavor the tender rice noodles, shrimp, and crisp bean sprouts to make an appetizing and filling meal-in-one noodle platter.

4 ounces rice stick noodles or vermicelli

1 pound medium raw shrimp, peeled, deveined, rinsed, and drained

2 tablespoons rice wine or sake

2 medium red onions, peeled

3 tablespoons olive or canola oil

1½ tablespoons good-quality Madras curry powder

2 tablespoons minced fresh ginger

SINGAPORE SAUCE (combine in a small bowl)

½ cup chicken broth, preferably low-sodium, or water

2 tablespoons soy sauce

½ teaspoon sugar

1 teaspoon salt

½ teaspoon freshly ground black pepper

3 cups bean sprouts, rinsed and drained

1. Soak the rice noodles in boiling water for 10 minutes, until softened. Slice the shrimp lengthwise in half along the back. Place in a bowl, add the rice wine, and toss lightly. Cut the onions in half, then cut into very thin, julienne slices.

2. Heat a wok or large skillet over high heat. Add 1 tablespoon of the oil and heat until very hot, about 15 seconds. Add the shrimp and stir-fry until cooked through, about 3 minutes. Remove and drain.

3. Wipe out the pan and reheat with the remaining 2 tablespoons oil over medium-high heat until very hot. Add the curry powder and stir-fry until fragrant, about 15 seconds. Add the red onions and minced ginger and stir-fry for about 2 minutes, until the onions are slightly limp. Add the Singapore Sauce and bring to a boil. Add the cooked shrimp, rice noodles, and bean sprouts and toss gently until the noodles have absorbed the sauce and are tender. Scoop onto a platter and serve.

VARIATIONS: *In the traditional recipe, barbecued pork is added with the shrimp. Use either, or the other, or both. Add different vegetables, such as 1 cup shredded Chinese cabbage, carrots, or mushrooms.*

For a stronger curry flavor, add another ½ tablespoon curry powder.

MING TSAI'S "NEW" FRIED RICE

6 TO 8 SERVINGS

Ming Tsai wears many hats: A celebrity PBS chef, owner of the award-winning Blue Ginger restaurant, and cookbook author. He is also a fellow member of the Nutrition Round Table at the Harvard School of Public Health. We featured this delicious and healthy rendition of shrimp fried rice on my video blog, www.spicesoflife.com.

1 pound raw baby or medium shrimp, peeled, deveined, rinsed, and drained

$\frac{1}{2}$ teaspoon kosher salt, or to taste

$\frac{1}{4}$ teaspoon freshly ground black pepper

7 scallions or 1 bunch, ends trimmed

3 tablespoons canola oil

2 tablespoons finely chopped garlic

2 tablespoons finely chopped fresh ginger

1 medium onion, cut into $\frac{1}{2}$-inch dice

2 cups grated or shredded carrots

4 ribs celery, cut into $\frac{1}{2}$-inch dice (about 1 cup)

6 cups shredded kale, stems and center ribs removed, cut into $\frac{1}{4}$-inch ribbons

4 cups leftover cooked brown rice, at room temperature

2 tablespoons soy sauce

1. Season the shrimp with the salt and pepper. Finely chop the white and green parts of the scallions and separate.

2. Heat a wok or large skillet over high heat. Add 2 tablespoons of the oil. Swirl to coat the pan. When the oil shimmers, add the shrimp and stir-fry just until pink, about 3 minutes. Remove with a handled strainer and drain.

3. Wipe the pan and heat with the remaining 1 tablespoon oil until very hot. Add the scallion whites, garlic, ginger, onion, carrots, celery, and kale and stir-fry until softened, about 2 to 4 minutes. Add the rice and shrimp and toss thoroughly until heated through. Add the soy sauce and toss. Taste for seasoning and adjust if necessary. Transfer to a platter and garnish with the scallion greens. Serve immediately.

CRISP FISH FILLETS WITH SWEET AND SOUR GLAZE

4 TO 6 SERVINGS

Tilapia is a reasonably priced, firm, meaty fish that is ideal for pan-frying. The texture remains crisp even after the fish is lightly coated with a sweet and sour glaze. The Monterey Bay Aquarium recommends buying U.S.-farmed tilapia and avoiding tilapia imported from Taiwan or China.

4 skinless tilapia fillets, 6 to 8 ounces each

2 1/2 tablespoons rice wine or sake

1 tablespoon minced ginger

1 red or orange bell pepper, cored and seeded

1/4 cup cornstarch or flour

3 1/2 tablespoons olive or canola oil

1 1/2 tablespoons minced garlic

1/2 pound snow or snap peas, ends snapped and veiny strings removed

SWEET AND SOUR GLAZE (combine in a small bowl)

9 tablespoons water

6 tablespoons ketchup

5 tablespoons clear rice vinegar

5 tablespoons firmly packed light brown sugar

1/2 teaspoon Sriracha hot sauce (optional)

3/4 teaspoon salt

1/4 teaspoon freshly ground black pepper

1. Rinse and drain the fish fillets and place in a bowl. Add the rice wine and ginger and rub all over the fillets to coat. Let sit briefly. Cut the peppers into 1-inch square pieces. Sprinkle the cornstarch on a plate. Lightly dredge the fish fillets in the cornstarch mixture and lay out on another plate.

2. Heat a large skillet over medium-high heat. Add 3 tablespoons of the oil and heat until very hot. Lay the fillets in the pan and fry for about 3 minutes on each side, until golden brown. (Frying time will vary depending on the thickness of the fish.) Remove and drain on paper towels. Arrange the fried fillets on a platter or serving plates.

3. Pour out any oil from the pan and reheat over medium-high heat until hot. Add the remaining 1/2 tablespoon oil. Add the garlic, peppers, and snow peas and toss lightly for 5 to 6 minutes, until crisp-tender. Add the Sweet and Sour Glaze and toss lightly to coat the vegetables. Spoon the sweet and sour vegetables over the fish and serve with rice.

> Substitute any firm-textured white fish for the tilapia,
> such as sea bass or red snapper.

GOLDEN SCALLION-GINGER SCALLOPS

4 TO 6 SERVINGS

An understated, simple sauce made with scallions and ginger can enhance and accentuate the flavor of fresh seafood and vegetables. This is especially true with scallops that have been pan-seared quickly until golden brown and stir-fried baby bok choy.

1 pound sea or bay scallops, muscles removed and rinsed and drained

1 teaspoon salt

1/4 teaspoon freshly ground black pepper

7 scallions, ends trimmed and discarded

1 1/4 pounds bok choy or baby bok choy, rinsed and drained

3 tablespoons olive or canola oil

3 tablespoons minced fresh ginger

1/2 cup rice wine or sake or very dry white wine

2 tablespoons fresh lemon juice

1 teaspoon toasted sesame oil

1. Rinse, drain, and blot the scallops dry with paper towels. Cut any large scallops in half horizontally. Season with the salt and pepper. Mince the white sections of the scallions and cut the greens into 1/2-inch lengths.

2. Remove any tough or wilted outer stalks from the bok choy and discard. Trim and discard the stem ends. If using regular bok choy, discard an inch of the leafy section and cut the stalks into thin slices about 1/4 inch thick. Cut the leafy sections into 1/2-inch pieces, keeping the leafy sections separate from the tougher ones. If using baby bok choy, cut the thicker hearts lengthwise in half. Put the bok choy in the sink in water to cover and rinse thoroughly, since they are often sandy. Drain thoroughly.

3. Heat a wok or large skillet over high heat. Add 2 tablespoons of the oil and heat until very hot, but not smoking. Pan-fry the scallops for about 2 1/2 minutes on each side, until golden brown. (If there are too many, fry in two batches.) Set the scallops aside, saving the pan juices.

4. Reheat the pan with the remaining 1 tablespoon oil over high heat until very hot. Add the ginger and scallion whites and stir-fry until fragrant, about 15 seconds. Add the scallion greens and the stalk sections of the regular bok choy or all the baby bok choy and toss lightly over high heat for a minute. Add the rice wine and cover. Cook for 3 to 4 minutes, until crisp-tender, stirring occasionally. If using regular bok choy, add the leafy sections now and continue cooking, uncovered, for 1 1/2 minutes, until crisp-tender.

(continued)

5. Add the cooked scallops, lemon juice, and toasted sesame oil and stir-fry over high heat until heated through. Scoop onto a platter and serve with rice or another whole grain.

VARIATION: *Substitute any type of fresh seafood (shrimp, lobster, clams, or firm-fleshed fish fillets) or chicken for the scallops, seared over high heat until golden brown and cooked through.*

Chinese doctors believe scallions are warming to the body,
and prescribe scallion tea (one bunch of finely chopped
whole scallions steeped in 1 pint of hot water) to
promote urination and sweating.

LEMONY CILANTRO CHICKEN
WITH SWISS CHARD

6 SERVINGS

This refreshing and basic lemony sauce seasoned with fresh cilantro and basil is superb with chicken, pork, and all types of seafood or tofu. You can pair other fresh herbs like chives, tarragon, or oregano with fresh parsley in place of the cilantro and basil.

1 pound boneless, skinless chicken breasts or thighs, trimmed of fat and gristle

2 tablespoons soy sauce

1 1/2 tablespoons minced fresh ginger

1 pound Swiss chard (1 bunch)

2 1/2 tablespoons olive or canola oil

2 1/2 tablespoons minced garlic

1 1/2 cups shredded or grated carrots

2 tablespoons rice wine or sake

HERB SAUCE (combine in a small bowl and stir until the sugar dissolves)

1/4 cup light soy sauce, or to taste

2 1/2 tablespoons freshly squeezed lemon juice, or to taste

1 1/2 tablespoons sugar, or to taste

1 1/2 tablespoons chopped stemmed fresh basil leaves

1 1/2 tablespoons stemmed cilantro leaves

1. Cut the chicken into 1/2-inch cubes. Place in a bowl, add the soy sauce and minced ginger, and toss lightly to coat. Trim the center ribs and the stems of the Swiss chard, discard, and coarsely chop the leaves (about 5 cups).

2. Heat a wok or heavy skillet over high heat. Add 1 tablespoon of the oil and heat until very hot. Add the chicken and cook for about 4 1/2 minutes, until opaque and cooked through. Remove with a slotted spoon and drain.

3. Reheat the pan with the remaining 1 1/2 tablespoons oil until very hot. Add the garlic, carrots, and rice wine and toss lightly. Partially cover and cook for about 30 seconds, until the carrots are tender. Uncover and add the cooked chicken, Swiss chard, and Herb Sauce. Toss lightly over high heat for 1 1/2 minutes, until everything is heated through and the Swiss chard is cooked. Spoon onto a serving platter and serve with rice or another whole grain.

SEARED BLACK BEAN CHICKEN
OVER CRISP NOODLES

4 TO 6 SERVINGS

Fermented, salted black beans and garlic are the basic seasoning for the popular Cantonese lobster sauce. Jarred black bean garlic sauce is now available in many mainstream supermarkets, but the saltiness may vary. Use it sparingly, then add more if necessary. Once opened, it will keep indefinitely in the refrigerator.

1 pound boneless, skinless chicken breasts or thighs, trimmed of fat and gristle

1½ tablespoons minced garlic

2 tablespoons soy sauce

1 medium red onion, peeled

2 red bell peppers, cored and seeded

¾ pound snow or snap peas

6 ounces whole wheat spaghetti or angel hair noodles

1 teaspoon toasted sesame oil

2½ tablespoons olive or canola oil

BLACK BEAN SEASONINGS (combine in a small bowl)

3 tablespoons fermented (salted) black beans, rinsed lightly and chopped finely, or black bean garlic sauce

2 tablespoons minced fresh ginger

1½ tablespoons minced garlic

1 teaspoon crushed red pepper flakes (optional)

SAUCE (combine in a small bowl)

2 cups chicken broth, preferably low-sodium

3 tablespoons soy sauce, or to taste

2½ tablespoons rice wine or sake

½ tablespoon sugar

2 tablespoons cornstarch

1. Cut the chicken into 1-inch squares. Place in a bowl, add the garlic and soy sauce, and toss lightly to coat. Cut the onion and peppers into thin julienne slices. Snap the ends off the snow or snap peas and remove any veiny strings.

2. Preheat the broiler. Bring 3 quarts of water to a boil in a large pot. Add the noodles and cook for slightly less time than directed on the package, until nearly tender. Drain in a colander and rinse to remove the starch. Drain thoroughly and toss with the toasted sesame oil and 1 teaspoon of the olive or canola oil. Spread the noodles out on a baking sheet and broil for 10 to 15 minutes on each side, until golden brown. Alternatively, you may pan-fry the unrinsed noodles

(continued)

in 2 tablespoons hot oil until golden brown. If you do this in advance, you may reheat in the oven at 200°F.

3. Heat a wok or heavy skillet over high heat. Add 1 tablespoon of the olive or canola oil and heat until very hot, about 25 seconds. Add the chicken and cook for about 4½ minutes, or until opaque and cooked through. Remove with a slotted spoon and drain.

4. Arrange the noodles in a large, deep serving dish or bowl. Wipe the pan and reheat with the remaining olive or canola oil over medium-high heat until very hot. Add the Black Bean Seasonings and stir-fry for 2 to 3 minutes over high heat. Add the onion, peppers, and snap peas and stir-fry for about 1 minute. Add the Sauce, partially cover, and bring to a boil, stirring occasionally to prevent lumps. Add the chicken and toss lightly to coat. Spoon the mixture over the noodles and serve immediately.

VARIATION: *Substitute top round, flank steak, center-cut pork loin, very firm tofu, shrimp, or scallops cut into slices for the chicken.*

STIR-FRIED TURKEY TENDERLOIN
IN OYSTER SAUCE

6 SERVINGS

Oyster sauce is one of the most versatile sauce bases and can be used for all types of protein. You can serve this dish with rice, couscous, or quinoa, or double the sauce (increasing the broth or water to 2½ cups) and serve over noodles.

1 pound boneless, skinless turkey breast cutlets, trimmed of fat and gristle

3 tablespoons soy sauce

2 tablespoons minced garlic

1 pound broccolini or broccoli

2½ tablespoons olive or canola oil

1½ tablespoons minced fresh ginger

½ cup water

OYSTER SAUCE (combine in a small bowl)

½ cup low-sodium chicken broth or water

3 tablespoons oyster sauce

1½ tablespoons rice wine or sake

1½ teaspoons sugar

1½ teaspoons cornstarch

1. Holding the knife at an angle to the cutting board, cut the turkey cutlets into thin pieces that are about 3 inches long and 1 inch wide. Mix with the soy sauce and garlic in a bowl.

2. Cut away the stem ends of the broccolini or broccoli and discard. If using broccolini, cut each stalk into 1-inch sections. If using broccoli, peel the tough skin from the stem and cut on the diagonal into 1-inch sections. Separate the large florets into bite-size sections.

3. Heat a wok or a skillet over high heat. Add 1½ tablespoons of the oil and heat until very hot. Add the turkey pieces and cook for 4 to 4½ minutes, until opaque and cooked through. Remove with a handled strainer and drain.

4. Wipe the pan and reheat with the remaining 1 tablespoon oil until very hot. Add the ginger and stir-fry until fragrant, about 15 seconds. Add the broccolini or broccoli and toss lightly over medium heat for a minute. Add the water, cover, and cook for about 4½ minutes, until just tender. Drain off any excess water and add the Oyster Sauce. Turn the heat to high and bring to a boil, stirring constantly to prevent lumps. When the sauce has thickened, add the cooked turkey. Toss lightly to coat and spoon onto a serving platter. Serve with rice or another whole grain.

VARIATION: *Use American, Chinese, or Italian broccoli rabe, bok choy, or cabbage (same cooking time as the broccolini), snow or snap peas (cook for 1 minute), or asparagus (cook for 8 minutes).*

SPICY SICHUAN-STYLE GREEN BEANS

4 TO 6 SERVINGS

This spicy Sichuanese sauce is equally delicious with broccoli, snow or snap peas, cauliflower, shelled edamame, or bok choy. I love the convenience of pretrimmed string beans.

1 pound ground chicken

2 tablespoons soy sauce

1 teaspoon toasted sesame oil

2 tablespoons olive or canola oil

SEASONINGS

¼ cup minced scallions, white parts only

3 tablespoons minced garlic

1¼ teaspoons hot chili paste with garlic or crushed red pepper flakes, or to taste

1½ pounds green beans, ends trimmed, rinsed, and drained

SAUCE (combine in a small bowl)

1½ cups chicken broth, preferably low-sodium, or water

3 tablespoons soy sauce

3 tablespoons rice wine or sake

1½ teaspoons cornstarch mixed with 1 tablespoon water

1. In a bowl, mix the ground chicken with the soy sauce and sesame oil. Cut the beans in half on an angle if they are large.

2. Heat a wok or deep skillet over medium-high heat. Add 1 tablespoon of the oil and heat until very hot. Add the ground chicken and cook, chopping and mashing the meat with a spatula to separate, until completely cooked. Remove with a slotted spoon and drain.

3. Wipe the pan and reheat. Add the remaining 1 tablespoon oil until very hot. Add the Seasonings and stir-fry briefly, about 15 seconds, then add the green beans. Stir-fry for about 1 minute over medium-high heat. Add the Sauce. Partially cover, bring to a boil, and cook for 7 to 8 minutes, until the beans are crisp-tender. Uncover, add the cooked chicken and the cornstarch and water mixture. Cook, stirring to prevent lumps, until thickened. Spoon onto a serving plate and serve with rice or another whole grain.

Chinese doctors believe that string beans strengthen the spleen, pancreas, and kidneys.

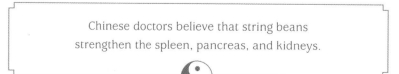

KUNG PAO PORK WITH SNOW PEAS

4 SERVINGS

This Sichuanese dish, which is usually made with chicken and peanuts, has become a stir-fry classic. Keep a jar of Kung Pao Sauce in the fridge and it's easy to add leftover grilled, pan-roasted, or steamed meat or seafood with a cooked vegetable of your choice and some rice or another grain for an instant meal-in-one dish.

1 pound boneless, center-cut pork loin, trimmed of fat and gristle

2 tablespoons soy sauce

1½ cups thinly sliced water chestnuts (about 8 ounces)

2½ tablespoons olive or canola oil

SEASONINGS

2½ tablespoons minced fresh ginger

2 tablespoons minced garlic

1 teaspoon hot chili paste or crushed red pepper flakes, or to taste

KUNG PAO SAUCE (combine in a small bowl)

¾ cup chicken broth or water

2½ tablespoons soy sauce

2 tablespoons rice wine or sake

1½ tablespoons Chinese black vinegar or Worcestershire sauce

1 teaspoon toasted sesame oil

2 teaspoons cornstarch

¾ pound snow or snap peas, ends snapped and veiny strings removed

1 cup dry-roasted salted almonds

1. Cut the pork into thin slices across the grain, then cut the slices lengthwise in half. Mix with the soy sauce and let sit while preparing the remaining ingredients, Blanch the water chestnuts for 10 seconds in boiling water, then refresh in cold water and drain.

2. Heat wok or a skillet over high heat. Add 1½ tablespoons of the oil and heat until very hot. Add the pork and cook for 4 to 5 minutes, until opaque and cooked through. Remove with a slotted spoon or strainer and drain.

3. Wipe the pan and heat with the remaining 1 tablespoon oil until hot. Add the Seasonings and stir-fry briefly, about 15 seconds. Add the water chestnuts and stir-fry over high heat for about 1½ minutes, until heated through. Add the Kung Pao Sauce and the snow or snap peas and cook, stirring continuously to prevent lumps, until thickened. Add the cooked pork and almonds and toss lightly to heat through. Spoon onto a serving dish or platter and serve with rice or another whole grain.

VARIATION: *Substitute boneless, skinless chicken fillets for the pork, shelled edamame or green beans for the snow peas, and dry roasted cashews or peanuts for the almonds.*

Almonds are one of the richest nonanimal sources of calcium and have been shown to reduce cholesterol.

SAUCY HOISIN PORK ROLL-UPS

6 SERVINGS

I love informal wrap dishes where stir-fried foods are scooped into lettuce, Mandarin pancakes, or flour tortillas and eaten with your hands. To save time, you can chop the water chestnuts coarsely in the food processor.

1 square (about 1 pound) extra-firm tofu

1 pound ground pork or chicken

2 tablespoons soy sauce

1½ cups water chestnuts (one 19-ounce can)

1 head Boston or leafy lettuce, rinsed and drained

1½ tablespoons olive or canola oil

3 tablespoons minced garlic

2 tablespoons minced fresh ginger

3 tablespoons minced scallions, white sections only

SAUCE (combine in a small bowl)

10 tablespoons hoisin sauce

4½ tablespoons water

2½ tablespoons soy sauce

1 pound frozen shelled edamame, defrosted

1. Cut the tofu horizontally in half and wrap in paper towels. Put a heavy weight, such as a pot, on top. Let drain while preparing the other ingredients, changing the towels once. Cut the tofu into ¼-inch dice. Place the ground meat in a shallow dish, add the soy sauce, and toss lightly.

2. Blanch the water chestnuts in boiling water for 10 seconds, refresh in cold water, and drain. Chop coarsely.

3. Trim and discard the core of the lettuce. Separate the leaves, trimming the stem ends, and flatten with a knife. Arrange in a serving bowl or basket.

4. Heat a wok or skillet over medium-high heat. Add ½ tablespoon of the oil and heat until very hot, about 15 seconds. Add the ground meat and stir-fry, mashing to break up the large pieces, until the meat changes color and is cooked through. Drain in a colander.

(continued)

5. Wipe the pan and reheat with the remaining 1 tablespoon oil until very hot. Add the minced garlic, ginger, and scallions and stir-fry until fragrant, about 15 seconds. Add the water chestnuts and toss lightly until heated through. Add the diced tofu and Sauce. Stir-fry to coat the tofu with the sauce, then cook, covered, for 1½ minutes. Uncover and continue cooking until the sauce has thickened. Add the cooked meat and edamame and toss to coat. Scoop onto a serving platter or bowl and serve with the lettuce. To serve, spoon some of the mixture into a lettuce leaf, roll it up, and eat with your fingers.

VARIATIONS: *For a vegetarian version, omit the meat and double the amount of tofu.*

Replace the ground pork with turkey or beef.

For extra spice, add 1 teaspoon chili paste with garlic or crushed red pepper flakes when you add the other seasonings in step 5.

Edamame is an excellent source of protein and fiber,
and it helps lower the risk of heart disease.

SPICY ORANGE BEEF

4 TO 6 SERVINGS

Vibrant seasonings like orange zest and red pepper flakes, along with tender slices of beef and shredded carrots, come together in an explosion of flavors. The crunchy texture of the water chestnuts complements the tender stalks of spinach. Serve with steamed rice to capture all the savory sauce.

1 pound top sirloin steak or flank steak, trimmed of fat and gristle

2 tablespoons soy sauce

1½ tablespoons minced fresh ginger

1 cup water chestnuts (one 8-ounce can), thinly sliced

3 tablespoons olive or canola oil

2 bags (6 to 8 ounces each) prewashed baby spinach

1 tablespoon minced garlic

1½ tablespoons rice wine or sake

¾ to 1 teaspoon salt

2 cups shredded or grated carrots

2½ tablespoons grated orange zest

1 teaspoon crushed red pepper flakes

SAUCE (combine in a small bowl)

⅓ cup water

3 tablespoons soy sauce

2 tablespoons rice wine or sake

1 tablespoon clear rice vinegar

½ teaspoon toasted sesame oil

¼ teaspoon freshly ground black pepper

2 teaspoons cornstarch

1. Cut the meat into 1-inch-wide strips, then cut each strip across the grain into thin slices. Mix the beef with the soy sauce and chopped ginger to coat. Blanch the sliced water chestnuts for 10 seconds in boiling water, then refresh in cold water and drain.

2. Heat a skillet or wok over high heat. Add ½ tablespoon of the oil and heat until very hot, but not smoking. Add the spinach, minced garlic, rice wine, and salt and stir-fry until the spinach is almost wilted. Scoop out of the pan and arrange around the edge of a serving platter.

3. Reheat the pan with 2 tablespoons of the oil over high heat until very hot, about 15 seconds, swirling the oil around the pan. Add the meat and stir-fry until the meat changes color and is cooked through, 3 to 4 minutes. Remove and drain in a colander.

4. Wipe the pan and reheat with the remaining ½ tablespoon oil until very hot. Add the blanched water chestnuts, carrots, orange zest, and red pepper flakes. Toss lightly over high heat for 1 or 2 minutes, until heated through. Add the Sauce and lower the heat to medium-high. Stir continuously to keep from forming lumps, until thickened. Add the cooked meat and toss lightly to coat. Spoon into the center of the platter with the spinach. Serve immediately with steamed rice.

CHAPTER 4

ASIAN GRILL

ASIAN GRILL

ALTHOUGH ASIAN COOKING is my specialty, I would be hard pressed to choose between stir-frying and grilling. It's not only the ease, convenience, and speed of cooking over an open fire that appeals to me. There's also the pungent, smoky tenderness of the cooked food. Another factor is the delicious leftovers. One of my most popular dinner staples is a stir-fry of sliced grilled meat or seafood and vegetables tossed together with a simple sauce and served with rice, quinoa, or couscous for a quick and satisfying weeknight meal.

Because I'm American, grilling is encoded in my DNA. Interestingly enough, however, there are many similarities between stir-frying and grilling. Since both accentuate the flavor of ingredients, only top-quality foods should be used. Also, like with stir-frying, organization is critical to the success of the finished dish. When grilling, the main protein (meat or seafood) is marinated. Marinades not only give additional flavor, but, according to research, they prevent the grilled food from producing cancer-causing compounds. And with both cooking techniques, the fire should be extremely hot to sear the ingredients, sealing in the flavor and natural juices.

Despite the fact that I live in New England, I grill throughout the year: Neither rain, sleet, nor snow can deter me from firing up my trusty gas Weber. (Some grilling purists may feel I've gone to the dark side, but you can't beat the speed or convenience of a gas grill, especially when you have a busy schedule.)

I've developed some standard marinades that I like to prepare in bulk and store in containers in the refrigerator. I do the same with different types of stir-fry sauces. Most can be used interchangeably with seafood, poultry, various meats, and vegetables. This decreases weeknight dinner prep time so that I can rustle up a delicious and healthy meal in minutes.

Exact grilling times of food are hard to predict. All the recipes have approximate cooking times, and here are some tips to test the food for doneness:

- Test for fish: Use a fork and knife to prod the cooked fillet or steak. The flesh should be firm, slightly flaky, and opaque when sliced through.

- Test for chicken: Make a cut in the meat with the tip of a sharp paring knife. The juice should be clear and the meat should be opaque with no trace of pink, especially at the bone.

- Touch and knife tests for meat: Meat generally becomes firmer as it cooks.

- Experienced chefs can judge the doneness by feeling the surface of the meat with the tip of the finger. Rare corresponds to the texture of the fleshy area between the thumb and forefinger, while medium-rare feels like the skin surface at the base of the thumb. The best method is to cut into the meat with the tip of a small paring knife to see the degree of doneness.

Whatever method you use, remove the food (particularly meat and seafood) from the fire just before it is done, as it will continue to cook after it is taken off the grill.

Unlike the other meal-in-one dishes in this book, the recipes in this chapter are meant to be paired with a selection from Whole Grains and Easy Sides (Chapter 5). I've made suggestions for specific sides for many of the grilled recipes, but feel free to mix and match. The main point is to plan a whole, balanced meal with a protein, vegetable(s), and staple food such as a whole grain. Enjoy!

ORANGE-MAPLE SALMON

4 SERVINGS

Salmon is a perfect fish to grill since it has a little fat that melts away with the intense heat, leaving the fish moist and tender. The ginger and maple in the marinade really bring out the smoky lushness of the salmon.

ORANGE-MAPLE SAUCE

1½ tablespoons orange zest

½ cup fresh orange juice

1½ tablespoons fresh lemon juice

¼ cup soy sauce

2 tablespoons maple syrup

1½ tablespoons minced fresh ginger

1 skin-on salmon fillet (about 1½ pounds) or 4 salmon steaks (about 1 inch thick and 6 ounces each), rinsed and drained

3 tablespoons olive or canola oil, or olive oil spray, for oiling the grill

1. To make the Orange-Maple Sauce: Mix all the ingredients in a saucepan and bring to a boil over medium-high heat. Reduce the heat slightly and simmer for 5 minutes. Pour half into a bowl and cool slightly. Keep the other half warm.

2. Arrange the salmon in one layer in a shallow pan, add the cooled sauce, and turn the fish so that all sides are coated. If using a fillet, place skin side up. Cover with plastic wrap and let marinate for 15 minutes.

3. Prepare a medium-hot fire for grilling or preheat a gas grill. Arrange a rack 3 to 4 inches from the heat. Brush or spray the grill rack with oil and arrange the salmon on the rack (skin side down if grilling a fillet). Grill until the flesh is just opaque, 6 to 7 minutes per side, brushing with the sauce left in the pan. Carefully slide the fish off the grill and serve with the remaining warm sauce spooned on top. Serve with Spicy Orange Fennel Slaw (page 125) or another of the Easy Sides in Chapter 5, and with rice or another whole grain.

VARIATION: *Substitute trout or any other firm-fleshed fish, such as halibut, swordfish, tilapia, or sea bass, for the salmon.*

GRILLED GINGER CHAR

4 SERVINGS

Arctic char is closely related to salmon, but the taste is even milder, making it a terrific fish to grill or pan-fry. One of my most popular marinades is the easiest and simplest to make with a little minced ginger, soy sauce, rice wine or sake, and toasted sesame oil.

1 skin-on arctic char fillet (about 1 inch thick and 1½ pounds), rinsed and drained

GINGER-SOY MARINADE (combine in a small bowl)

3 tablespoons soy sauce

2 tablespoons rice wine or sake

1½ tablespoons minced ginger

½ teaspoon toasted sesame oil

1. Arrange the char in one layer in a shallow pan. Pour the Ginger-Soy Marinade over the fish and turn so that all sides are coated. Place the fish skin side up, cover with plastic wrap, and let marinate for 15 minutes.

2. Prepare a medium-hot fire for grilling, or preheat a gas grill. Arrange an oiled rack 3 to 4 inches from the heat. Arrange the char, skin side down, on the rack. Grill until the flesh is just opaque, 6 to 7 minutes per side, brushing with the marinade remaining in the pan. Carefully slide the fish off the grill and carefully peel away the skin and discard. Cut into 4 sections. Serve with Sake-Roasted Brussels Sprouts (page 126) or another one of the Easy Sides in Chapter 5, and with rice or another whole grain.

VARIATION: *This all-purpose marinade is excellent for salmon, trout, halibut, other types of seafood, and chicken.*

> Similar to salmon, Arctic char is a great source of omega-3 fatty acids that strengthen the heart and prevent cardiovascular disease.

BALSAMIC-SOY SWORDFISH

6 SERVINGS

Swordfish is one of my family's favorite fish for grilling, but because it may contain high levels of mercury, we limit our consumption to no more than once every two weeks. If there are any leftovers, the cold grilled fish is delicious in a salad. The all-purpose marinade may be used for all types of seafood, chicken, and vegetables.

BALSAMIC-SOY MARINADE (combine in a small bowl)

- 2 1/2 tablespoons balsamic vinegar
- 2 tablespoons soy sauce
- 1 1/2 tablespoons minced fresh ginger

1 1/2 pounds swordfish steak (1 to 1 1/2 inches thick) or firm-fleshed fish fillets such as tilapia, red snapper, or mahimahi, rinsed lightly and drained

2 tablespoons olive or canola oil, or olive oil spray, for oiling the grill

1. Combine the Balsamic-Soy Marinade and fish in a shallow dish; turn the fish to coat. Let marinate while the fire is heating.

2. Prepare a medium-hot fire for grilling, or preheat a gas grill. Arrange a rack about 3 inches from the heat. Brush or spray the grill rack with oil and place the fish on the rack. Cover and grill, basting with the marinade, until the meat is opaque, 7 to 8 minutes on each side depending on the thickness of the fish.

3. Carefully slide the fish off the grill and cut into 6 portions. Serve with Lemony Edamame (page 127) or another one of the Easy Sides in Chapter 5, and with rice or another whole grain.

SCALLION-GINGER SEA BASS

4 SERVINGS

Chinese chefs believe if you buy very fresh fish, simple seasonings such as an easy scallion-ginger flavored oil will accentuate the natural sweet flavor of the seafood. Marinated briefly and grilled over a hot fire, this bass is superb.

4 scallions, ends trimmed

$1/4$ cup olive or canola oil

8 slices fresh ginger, smashed with the flat side of a knife

$1\frac{1}{2}$ pounds striped bass fillets (about 1-inch thick) or other firm fish fillets such as halibut, grouper, or swordfish, rinsed and drained

$1/3$ cup rice wine or sake

1 teaspoon salt

$1/2$ teaspoon freshly ground black pepper

1. Cut the scallions into 1-inch sections and smash with the flat side of a knife or cleaver. Heat the oil in a heavy saucepan with a lid over medium-high heat until very hot, 15 to 20 seconds. Add the scallions and ginger slices and stir-fry until fragrant, about 15 seconds. Remove from the heat, cover, and let cool.

2. Place the sea bass in a bowl. Add the scallion-ginger oil, rice wine, salt, and pepper. Rub the surface of the fillets with the flavored oil, cover with plastic wrap, and let marinate for 15 minutes.

3. Prepare a medium-hot fire for grilling, or preheat a gas grill. Arrange a rack 3 to 4 inches from the heat. Arrange the fish fillets on the rack, cover, and grill for 4 to 5 minutes per side, until the flesh is opaque. Slide the fillets off the grill and onto a platter or individual plates. Serve with Grilled Lemon-Soy Zucchini (page 130), Roasted Cherry Tomato-Cilantro Salsa (page 134), or another one of the Easy Sides in Chapter 5, and with brown rice or another whole grain.

TERIYAKI HALIBUT

4 SERVINGS

Once cooked, the juices of the seafood and the ginger-teriyaki sauce combine to make a splendid sauce. Supermarkets offer a variety of bottled teriyaki marinades, but I have yet to taste one as good as the one I've created.

GINGER-TERIYAKI SAUCE

- 1/3 cup soy sauce
- 1/3 cup water
- 1/3 cup rice wine or sake
- 7 tablespoons sugar
- 1 1/2 tablespoons minced fresh ginger
- 1 1/2 tablespoons cornstarch

- 1 1/2 pounds halibut steaks (1 to 1 1/2 inches thick) or other firm-fleshed fish fillets such as tilapia or swordfish, rinsed and drained
- 2 tablespoons olive or canola oil, or olive oil spray, for oiling the grill

1. To make the Ginger-Teriyaki Sauce: Mix all the ingredients in a heavy, medium-size saucepan. Cook over medium heat until thickened, stirring constantly with a wooden spoon to prevent lumps. Pour half into a bowl and let cool slightly. Keep the other half warm.

2. Arrange the fish in one layer in a shallow pan, add the cooled sauce, and turn the fish so that all sides are coated. Let marinate 15 minutes.

3. Prepare a medium-hot fire for grilling, or preheat a gas grill. Arrange a rack 3 to 4 inches from the heat. Brush or spray the grill rack with oil and arrange the fish on the rack. Cover and grill until the flesh is opaque, 5 to 6 minutes per side, depending on the thickness. Carefully slide the fish off the grill. Spoon some of the warm sauce on top of the fish. Serve with Seared Baby Bok Choy (page 129) or another of the Easy Sides in Chapter 5, and with brown rice or another whole grain.

VARIATION: *For an extra spicy sauce, add 1 teaspoon hot chili paste or crushed red pepper flakes.*

GRILLED MISO TUNA

4 SERVINGS

The saltiness and buttery texture of miso paste is a perfect match for the fresh, slightly briny flavor of tuna and other seafood. It's no surprise that it's a great base for a seafood marinade.

MISO MARINADE (combine in a small bowl)

$\frac{1}{3}$ cup sweet white miso paste (*miso shiro*)

$\frac{1}{3}$ cup rice wine or sake

$1\frac{1}{2}$ tablespoons minced fresh ginger

1 tablespoon fresh lemon juice

1 tablespoon sugar

1 teaspoon toasted sesame oil

4 very fresh tuna steaks (about 1 inch thick and 6 ounces each), rinsed and drained

3 tablespoons olive or canola oil, or olive oil spray, for oiling the grill

2 tablespoons minced scallion greens (optional)

1. Pour the Miso Marinade into a shallow dish, add the fish steaks, and turn to coat. Marinate for 15 to 20 minutes.

2. Prepare a medium-hot fire for grilling or preheat a gas grill. Arrange a rack about 3 inches from the heat. Remove the fish from the marinade, spreading the marinade with your hands so that there is a light coating. Brush or spray the grill rack with oil and arrange the fish steaks on the rack. Cover and grill for about $3\frac{1}{2}$ to 4 minutes on each side for rare, or 5 minutes each side for medium-rare, or more or less depending on the thickness of the steaks. Carefully slide the fish off the grill, arrange on individual plates, and sprinkle with the scallions (if using). Serve with Sweet and Sour Cucumbers (page 132) or another of the Easy Sides in Chapter 5, and with rice or another whole grain.

> Miso not only provides a rich, subtle flavor but is also extremely healthful. Because it is made from soybeans, it is believed to lower the risk of heart disease, reduce menopausal symptoms, and prevent cancer. It also aids digestion.

SPICY SKEWERED SHRIMP

4 TO 6 SERVINGS

Although pairing barbecued shrimp with fruit or vegetable salsa is not a classic Chinese practice, the two foods complement one another beautifully. I love to serve them together, wrapped in a Mandarin pancake or flour tortilla brushed lightly with toasted sesame oil. Then again, it's also nice to serve the shrimp with any of the Easy Sides (Chapter 5) and rice.

1¼ pounds raw large shrimp, peeled, deveined, rinsed, and drained

SPICY MARINADE

2 or 3 small hot red Thai peppers (see note below)

6 cloves peeled garlic, smashed with the flat side of a knife

¼ cup rice wine or sake

1 teaspoon toasted sesame oil

10-inch bamboo skewers (6), soaked in water for 1 hour and drained

1 tablespoon olive or canola oil, or olive oil spray, for oiling the grill

1. Using a sharp knife, score the shrimp lengthwise down the back so that they will butterfly when cooked. Place in a bowl.

2. To make the Spicy Marinade: Trim the ends of the peppers, remove the seeds, and cut into thin slices. Combine the peppers with the remaining marinade ingredients. Toss lightly with the shrimp, cover, and marinate briefly at room temperature or overnight in the refrigerator.

3. Thread the shrimp onto the skewers so that they lie flat.

4. Prepare a medium-hot fire for grilling or preheat a gas grill. Arrange a rack about 3 inches from the heat. Brush or spray the grill rack with oil and arrange the skewered shrimp on the rack. Grill for 3 to 4 minutes per side, basting with the marinade, until the shrimp are cooked through. Remove the shrimp from the skewers and serve with Roasted Cherry Tomato-Cilantro Salsa (page 134), or another of the Easy Sides in Chapter 5, and with rice or another whole grain.

NOTE: *If fresh red peppers are unavailable, you may substitute dried. Soften in hot water for 15 minutes and drain.*

MR. JIMMY'S BARBECUED CHICKEN

6 SERVINGS

Jimmy Toabe is the husband of my late mom's best friend, and he is a master griller. He would often make this dish for my family and other friends when we visited his family "camp," or cottage, on a pond in New Hampshire. It has now become one of my family's favorite meals for weeknights and entertaining. I am famous among my son's friends for my barbecued chicken and I owe it all to "Mr. Jimmy." Be sure to use a bottled dressing that is not overly sweet.

MARINADE

1 bottle (12 ounces) Italian salad dressing (1½ cups)

½ cup ketchup

2½ tablespoons soy sauce

2 tablespoons minced garlic

1½ pounds boneless, skinless chicken thighs, trimmed of fat and gristle

2 tablespoons olive or canola oil, or olive oil spray, for oiling the grill

1. Combine the Marinade ingredients in a bowl and add the chicken thighs. Stir to coat, cover with plastic wrap, and marinate in the refrigerator for several hours or overnight.

2. Prepare a medium-hot fire for grilling or preheat a gas grill. Arrange a rack 3 to 4 inches from the heat. Brush or spray the grill rack with oil and arrange the thighs on the rack. Cover and grill the chicken for 7 to 9 minutes per side, or until opaque and cooked through. To test, pierce with a knife and, if the juice is clear, the thighs are cooked. Slide off the grill onto a platter and serve with Asian Hot and Sour Slaw (page 137), or another one of the Easy Sides in Chapter 5, and with rice or another whole grain.

TANDOORI CHICKEN SLIDERS

4 SERVINGS

Grilled chicken burgers are stuffed into whole wheat pitas and topped with a healthy dollop of raita, a simple yogurt-based sauce seasoned lightly with ground cumin and fresh cilantro. The Tandoori Seasonings are not only excellent with ground chicken, but are equally delicious as a flavoring for boneless chicken parts, lamb (whole and ground), and seafood.

1 pound ground chicken or turkey

1 1/2 pounds shredded carrots

TANDOORI SEASONINGS

2 tablespoons minced fresh ginger

1 1/2 tablespoons minced garlic

1 teaspoon crushed red pepper flakes, or to taste

1 teaspoon ground cumin

1 teaspoon dried oregano

1 teaspoon salt

1/2 teaspoon freshly ground black pepper

2 tablespoons olive or canola oil, or olive oil spray, for oiling the grill

Simple Raita (page 138)

2 large whole wheat pitas, halved crosswise

2 cups assorted prewashed salad greens

Sliced tomatoes and/or avocados (optional)

1. Combine the ground chicken and carrots in a bowl, add the Tandoori Seasonings, and mix. Dipping your hands in water to prevent the chicken from sticking, shape the mixture into eight 3/4-inch-thick patties. Arrange on a plate that has been brushed with oil and refrigerate.

2. Prepare a medium-hot fire for grilling, or preheat a gas grill. Arrange a rack 3 to 4 inches from the heat. Brush or spray the rack with oil and arrange the patties on the rack. Cover and grill for 4 to 5 minutes per side, until cooked through. Remove to a platter and let sit for a few minutes.

3. While the chicken burgers are grilling, toast the pitas on the grill for a few minutes on each side, or wrap in a damp towel and microwave for 1 minute.

4. To serve, stuff two burgers into a pita, add some greens on top, and spoon some raita into the sandwich. Serve the extra raita on the side in a serving bowl.

VIETNAMESE CHICKEN WITH CILANTRO VINAIGRETTE

6 TO 8 SERVINGS

3 whole chicken breasts on the bones
(about 2 pounds)

VIETNAMESE MARINADE

1 lime

1 stalk lemongrass, ends trimmed
and tough outer husks removed, or
1½ teaspoons grated lemon zest

2 tablespoons chopped garlic

1½ tablespoons soy sauce

CILANTRO VINAIGRETTE

½ cup plus 1 tablespoon soy sauce

6 tablespoons rice vinegar

3 tablespoons sugar

2 tablespoons mirin or 2 tablespoons
rice wine plus 1 tablespoon sugar

3 tablespoons chopped cilantro leaves

½ pound sugar snap peas, ends trimmed
and veiny strings removed

3 cups peeled and grated or shredded
carrots

1. Trim the chicken breasts of any fat or gristle and place on a plate.

2. Remove the peel from the lime (reserving the flesh) and drop the peel into the feed tube of a food processor along with the remaining Vietnamese Marinade ingredients in the order listed. Blend to a paste and rub the mixture all over the chicken breasts. (If you like, you can carefully work your fingers under the skin of the chicken breast and spread some of the seasonings over the breast meat.)

3. Prepare a medium-hot fire for grilling, or preheat a gas grill and arrange a rack 3 to 4 inches from the heat. Brush the grill with the oil and arrange the breasts on the grill. Grill covered for about 7 to 9 minutes per side, or until the chicken is opaque and cooked through. To test, pierce with a knife and, if the juice is clear, they are cooked. Slide off the grill onto a platter. Let the chicken rest for 5 minutes, then slice the meat off the bones, cutting thinly across the grain.

4. While the chicken is grilling, combine the Cilantro Vinaigrette ingredients in a bowl. Taste for seasonings, adding juice from the reserved lime to taste and more cilantro if you like.

4. Bring 2 quarts water in a saucepan to a boil. Add the snap peas, blanch for 15 seconds, drain and refresh in cold water. Drain again, Sprinkle the snap peas in the center of a platter and make a ring of carrots around the peas. Make a little well in the center for the chicken and spoon some of the cilantro vinaigrette on top. Pass the remainder in a small bowl.

FIVE-SPICE PORK TENDERLOIN

4 SERVINGS

Five-spice powder—a mixture of star anise, powdered licorice root, cinnamon, cloves, and fennel—is now available widely in most supermarkets in the spice aisle. It is a pungent seasoning perfectly suited for pork, chicken, lamb, and duck.

1¼ pounds pork tenderloin, trimmed of fat and gristle

FIVE-SPICE MARINADE (combine in a small bowl)

    3 tablespoons soy sauce

    3 tablespoons rice wine or sake

    1½ tablespoons minced fresh ginger

    1½ tablespoons minced garlic

    1½ teaspoons sugar

    1 teaspoon toasted sesame oil

    1 teaspoon crushed red pepper flakes (optional)

    1 teaspoon five-spice powder (see note below)

2 tablespoons olive or canola oil, or olive oil spray, for oiling the grill

1. Place the pork in a shallow dish, pour the Five-Spice Marinade over it, and rub to coat. Cover with plastic wrap and marinate in the refrigerator for several hours or overnight.

2. Prepare a medium-hot fire for grilling or preheat a gas grill. Arrange a rack 3 to 4 inches from the heat. Brush or spray the grill rack with oil and arrange the pork on the rack. Cover and grill for 9 to 10 minutes on each side, or until the internal temperature registers 145°F. Transfer to a cutting board and let rest 5 minutes, then cut into thin slices, about ¼ inch thick. Serve with Smoky Sesame Corn on the Cob (page 141), or another of the Easy Sides in Chapter 5, and with rice or another whole grain.

> The seasonings in five-spice powder, including star anise, cinnamon, and fennel, aid digestion, particularly in helping the body to digest meat. For a substitute, see page xiv.

GRILLED GARLIC STEAK TIPS

4 TO 6 SERVINGS

When it comes to grilling steak, my philosophy is to keep it simple. High-quality meat needs hardly any seasoning—although I do admit to a preference for lots of garlic and a touch of sugar to help to caramelize the meat.

7 scallions, ends trimmed

1½ pounds sirloin tip, trimmed and cut into 1-inch chunks

6 tablespoons soy sauce

2 tablespoons minced garlic

1 scant teaspoon sugar

10-inch bamboo skewers (6), soaked in water to cover for 1 hour and drained

2 tablespoons olive or canola oil, or olive oil spray, for oiling the grill

1. Cut the scallions into 1½-inch lengths. Mix the beef with the soy sauce, garlic, and sugar. Toss lightly to coat and cover with plastic wrap. Marinate briefly at room temperature or overnight in the refrigerator.

2. Alternate threading the beef and scallion pieces on the skewers.

3. Prepare a medium-hot fire for grilling or preheat a gas grill. Arrange a rack about 3 inches from the heat. Brush or spray the grill rack with oil and arrange the skewered beef on the rack. Grill for 5 to 6 minutes per side for medium-rare. Serve with Balsamic-Ginger Roasted Sweet Potato Fries (page 130), Smoky Sesame Corn on the Cob (page 141), or another of the Easy Sides in Chapter 5, and with rice or another whole grain.

SPICY HOISIN LAMB KEBABS WITH MULTI-COLORED PEPPERS AND ONIONS

4 TO 6 SERVINGS

1½ pounds lamb kebabs, boneless leg of lamb, or top round of lamb, trimmed of fat and gristle

3 red or orange bell peppers, cored and seeded

2 medium red onions, peeled

10-inch bamboo skewers (8), soaked in water to cover for 1 hour and drained

HOISIN MARINADE (combine in a small bowl)

½ cup hoisin sauce

⅓ cup soy sauce

6 tablespoons rice wine or sake

2 tablespoons chopped garlic

1½ tablespoons sugar

2 tablespoons olive or canola oil, or olive oil spray, for oiling the grill

1. If not using kebabs, cut the lamb into 1½-inch squares. Cut the peppers into pieces about the same size as the meat. Cut the red onions in half, then quarters, and separate the pieces.

2. Alternate threading the lamb, peppers, and onion sections on the skewers. Arrange on a baking sheet and pour the Hoisin Marinade over the meat and vegetables, turning them to coat. Cover with plastic wrap and marinate briefly at room temperature or overnight in the refrigerator.

3. Prepare a medium-hot fire for grilling or preheat a gas grill. Arrange a rack about 3 inches from the heat. Brush or spray the grill rack with oil and arrange the skewers on the rack. Grill for 5 to 6 minutes per side for medium-rare. Serve with Balsamic-Ginger Roasted Sweet Potato Fries (page 139), or another of the Easy Sides in Chapter 5, and rice or another whole grain.

CHAPTER 5

ഗ∞ര

WHOLE GRAINS AND EASY SIDES

WHOLE GRAINS AND EASY SIDES

I'M NOT EMBARRASSED to admit that I used to be a white rice elitist. The thought of brown rice was not the least bit enticing, and forget about other whole grains. That was before I tasted the addictive flavor of brown basmati rice and the deliciously nutty taste of quinoa, and now I can't rave enough about whole wheat couscous. It may not be traditional to pair these grains with Asian dishes, but they complement them beautifully.

Asians have always relished grains and, according to custom, rice, noodles, or some form of grain makes up the bulk of the meal with vegetables, seafood, and meat dishes served as a garnish. Initially, this style of eating was foreign to me and I worried that I would gain weight. In fact, quite the opposite occurred: I not only lost weight, but I was less likely to become hungry between meals. (Among the many health-giving benefits of fiber in grains is that it satisfies your appetite and slows digestion.) For me, it initiated a new way of planning and eating meals that I still practice today with my family.

I am not alone. American cooks now are not only acknowledging the healthy benefits of whole grains, they are also finding that with a little creativity and by adding pungent spices, fresh herbs, and selected ethnic condiments, these foods can be transformed into sumptuous dishes that are excellent for weeknight meals and entertaining guests.

The selection of grains in supermarkets has never been more diverse or exciting. On your next visit, just take a look. The rice section alone is enormous, with most stores offering a choice of short- and long-grain varieties, wild rice, and different rice and grain blends. Personally, I prefer long-grain rices such as jasmine and basmati. Once cooked, they have a dry, fluffy texture and nutty flavor. Brown basmati takes longer to cook but is just as delicious. In addition, there's quinoa (which takes on a nutty flavor once it has been sautéed in a little oil), regular couscous, and whole wheat couscous. These last staples might not traditionally be served with Asian-influenced dishes, but I think they are excellent for rounding out a meal. To save time and plan efficiently for future dinners, I usually make a large batch of whatever grain I am preparing. Once it's cooked, I divide it up into smaller portions for freezing, then defrost a package prior to the meal to reheat briefly in the microwave or in a steamer.

As with grains, my "easy side" vegetable repertoire used to be pretty limited. Perhaps it reflected the paltry offerings in local supermarkets. But once I traveled to Asia and Europe and saw the exquisite offerings of vibrantly colored fresh fruits and vegetables available at open-air markets, I was inspired to create numerous dishes.

As I discovered, if you are cooking with superb-quality, seasonal vegetables fresh from the garden or farmers' market, less is more. In many cases, just a sprinkling of chopped garlic or fresh ginger, a drop of virgin olive oil, a little balsamic or rice vinegar or wine, and a pinch of salt combined with high temperature roasting, grilling, or stir-frying intensifies the intrinsic flavors and often caramelizes the natural sugars.

Try making some Sake-Roasted Brussels Sprouts, Grilled Lemon-Soy Zucchini, or Seared Baby Bok Choy. These are ridiculously easy, fast, and simple dishes, yet you will never tire of them. I like to make a large batch at the beginning of the week and reheat a portion in a microwave, steam, or pan-fry on subsequent nights when I am pressed for time.

Other recipes in this chapter include pungently flavored slaws, pickles, and salsas. They are not only superb with soups and stews, but they are especially delicious paired with grilled foods where their tart and often fruity flavors provide a delectable counterpoint to the smokiness of the barbecue. Just try a mouthful of Asian Hot and Sour Slaw paired with Orange-Maple Salmon or Chunky Avocado Salsa with Mr. Jimmy's Barbecued Chicken and I guarantee you will be hooked.

In addition to their delectable flavors, these dishes add color to the plate and a dose of good health to the body. Research has proven definitively that eating a variety of assorted fruits and vegetables can strengthen our immune system, reduce the risk of common diseases, increase our longevity, and help us lose weight. Since the recipes are so quick and easy, even the most harried cook can fit them into a busy schedule.

WHITE RICE

MAKES 6 CUPS

I prefer the fragrant and drier long-grain varieties of white rice, such as basmati and jasmine, which are now easily found in supermarkets. And my *new* secret with this book is the fabulous results I get from cooking rice in a microwave. It's terrific and requires no pots. Just use a soufflé dish or any heatproof bowl with a plate on top. Remember that the rice will continue cooking even after being removed from the heat.

2 cups long-grain rice such as jasmine or basmati

3 $\frac{1}{4}$ cups cold water

To make conventional boiled rice: Put the rice in a bowl and, using your fingers as a rake, rinse under cold running water to remove some of the talc. Drain in a strainer. Combine the rice and water in a heavy, 2-quart saucepan with a lid. Bring to a boil, cover, and reduce the heat to low. Simmer for 14 to 15 minutes, until the water has evaporated and craters appear on the surface. Remove from the heat and fluff lightly with a fork to separate the grains. Cover and let sit for 5 minutes. Serve immediately. (Or, if using for fried rice or a pilaf, spread out in a thin layer on a tray, let cool completely, cover with plastic wrap, and chill in the refrigerator overnight.)

To make the rice in a microwave: Rinse and drain as above, then transfer to a 3-quart soufflé dish or heatproof bowl. Add the water. Cover with an oven-safe plate or microwave cover and place in the microwave. Microwave on high for 12 minutes, or until just cooked. Remove from the microwave, fluff lightly with a fork, and let sit, covered, for 5 minutes. To save even more time, use a microwave rice cooker and follow the manufacturer's instructions.

Chinese doctors believe that rice strengthens the spleen
and pancreas and is soothing to the stomach. It also increases
the body's *qi*, or energy. A diet of rice gruel is prescribed
for digestive disorders and fevers.

BROWN RICE

MAKES 6 CUPS

Brown rice is now widely sold in all supermarkets and there are a number of different varieties, including long-grain basmati and short-grain rice. As with white rice, I prefer basmati for its fragrant flavor and drier texture. I like to cook large quantities and let it cool, then bag it in 2-cup portions and freeze to have on hand. Place in a bowl with waxed paper on top and microwave on full power for 3 minutes to defrost.

2 1/2 cups long-grain basmati brown rice

4 1/4 cups water

To make conventional boiled rice: Put the rice in a pot and, using your fingers as a rake, rinse under cold running water. Drain in a strainer. Combine the rice and 4 1/2 cups water in a heavy saucepan with a lid. Bring to a boil, cover, and reduce the heat to low. Simmer for 40 to 50 minutes, until the rice is just tender. Remove from the heat and fluff lightly with a fork to separate the grains. If the rice is wet or there is still water, drain the rice in a strainer, put back into the pot, and cover. Serve hot or warm. (Or, if using for fried rice or a pilaf, spread out in a thin layer on a tray, then let cool completely, cover with plastic wrap, and chill in the refrigerator overnight.)

To make the rice in a microwave: Rinse and drain the rice as above. Place the rice in a large, heatproof bowl with 6 cups water. Cover with an oven-safe plate or a microwave cover and place in the microwave. Microwave on high until the water boils, 8 to 10 minutes, depending on the microwave. Carefully remove the plate or cover and continue cooking for 20 minutes, or until most of water is absorbed. Remove from the microwave, cover, and let sit until any remaining water is absorbed. Fluff the rice with a fork and serve.

> Brown rice is rich in fiber, potassium, magnesium, and vitamins B_1, B_3, and B_6. It may help reduce the risk of colon cancer.

BASIC RECIPES FOR OTHER SELECTED WHOLE GRAINS

The following cooking times are approximate, and should be used as guidelines only, as recommended cooking times and quantities of water vary with different manufacturers and depend on whether the grain is processed. Make certain to check the label.

GRAIN	WATER	SUGGESTED COOKING TIME
1 cup long-grain brown rice	$1\frac{3}{4}$ cups	45 to 50 minutes (see recipe, page 113)
1 cup cracked kasha	2 cups	Toast, then add water and boil for 15 minutes
1 cup bulgur, medium grind*	$1\frac{1}{2}$ cups	15 minutes
1 cup cracked wheat**	$2\frac{1}{2}$ cups	Cover with boiling water and let stand 15 minutes
1 cup quinoa	$1\frac{1}{2}$ cups	Toast, then add water and boil for 15 minutes
1 cup wheat berries***	2 to 3 cups	1 to 2 hours

   * Traditional Middle Eastern bulgur is sold at ethnic markets. It is usually available in three types of grind: coarse, medium, and fine.

  ** Cracked wheat is more thoroughly milled than bulgur and is now sold in supermarkets. This should not be confused with bulgur.

*** Wheat berries (hard and soft) are sold in natural food stores and Middle Eastern markets. The cooking time will vary according to the variety.

NINA'S FRAGRANT RICE

6 SERVINGS

I love the subtle, nutty flavor of plain basmati and jasmine rice, but when I want to dress up a meal—anything from roasted or barbecued chicken to steamed or grilled seafood or meat—I add some seasonings to the rice to make it special.

3 scallions, ends trimmed

2 cups white jasmine or basmati rice

2 teaspoons fruity extra-virgin olive oil

2 tablespoons minced fresh ginger

3 1/4 cups water

1 tablespoon soy sauce

1 teaspoon toasted sesame oil

2 tablespoons toasted sesame seeds (optional)

1. Mince the white and green parts of the scallions separately.

2. Put the rice in a bowl and, using your fingers as a rake, rinse under cold running water to remove some of the talc. Drain in a strainer.

3. Heat the oil in a heavy 2-quart saucepan with a lid over medium-high heat until very hot. Add the minced scallion whites and the ginger and stir-fry for about 15 seconds, until very fragrant. Add the rice and water and bring to a boil. Reduce the heat to low, cover, and simmer for 14 to 15 minutes, until the water has evaporated and craters appear on the surface.

4. Remove from the heat and add the soy sauce, sesame oil, and sesame seeds, if using. Fluff lightly with a fork to separate the grains. Cover and let sit for 5 minutes. Garnish with the scallion greens and serve.

VARIATION: *For fragrant brown rice, use 2 1/2 cups long-grain brown basmati rice and 4 1/4 cups water. Follow the recipe as directed above, but cook the rice for 40 to 50 minutes.*

FRESH HERBED RICE

6 SERVINGS

The legendary Mediterranean food authority Claudia Roden first introduced me to the idea of adding fresh chopped herbs to rice just after it has been cooked to heighten the flavor. It is a simple yet crucial tip that elevates a mundane side dish to the sublime and brightens any meal.

4 cups just-cooked basmati or jasmine rice (see page 112)

HERB SEASONINGS

1 1/2 cups minced scallion greens

1 1/4 cups fresh dill sprigs, rinsed, drained, blotted dry, and chopped

1 cup fresh cilantro leaves, rinsed, drained, blotted dry, and chopped

2 1/2 tablespoons fruity olive oil

1 1/2 teaspoons salt, or to taste

3 tablespoons fresh lemon juice (optional)

Remove the cooked rice from the heat and immediately combine with the Herb Seasonings. Fluff the cooked rice lightly with a fork to separate the grains and mix the seasonings evenly. Cover and let stand for 10 minutes. Serve warm, at room temperature, or cold.

VARIATION: *You can vary the type of herbs you use, depending on what's available. Chopped fresh basil, chives, chervil, and tarragon are all excellent in place of the cilantro. To add a note of freshness, add 1 cup coarsely chopped flat parsley leaves.*

Dill enhances the secretion of digestive juices and eases flatulence and colic.

LEMON RICE

6 SERVINGS

I first tasted lemon rice when I studied with the brilliant chef Suresh Vaidyanathan from southern India. I've since adapted his recipe to make a more subtle, streamlined version. It's so light and refreshing that I often serve it as a side dish with any type of food.

2 teaspoons olive or canola oil

1½ teaspoons grated lemon zest (from ½ lemon)

½ teaspoon ground turmeric

4 cups cooked basmati or jasmine rice (see page 112), cooled to room temperature

2 tablespoons fresh lemon juice

1 teaspoon salt, or to taste

Heat the oil in a heavy wok or skillet until very hot, about 20 seconds. Add the lemon zest and turmeric and stir-fry for about 1 minute, until very fragrant. Add the rice and, using your spatula, mash and separate the grains over medium heat so the rice will heat evenly. Once hot, stir in the lemon juice and salt and heat through, tossing lightly. Taste for seasoning, adding more salt or lemon juice if necessary. Spoon into a serving bowl and serve.

CARDAMOM-COCONUT RICE

6 SERVINGS

Most coconut rice recipes are rather heavy and labor intensive since they use coconut milk, which requires constant mixing while cooking to prevent it from separating. This recipe was inspired by one in Didi Emmons's *Entertaining for a Veggie Planet*. It is really easy to prepare, light, and excellent served with a curry or any spicy dish.

2 cups white basmati or jasmine rice

3½ cups water

¾ cup dried unsweetened coconut

4 cardamom pods, smashed lightly with the flat side of a knife

1 teaspoon salt

1. Put the rice in a bowl and, using your fingers as a rake, rinse under cold running water to remove some of the talc. Drain in a strainer.

2. Combine the rice, water, coconut, cardamom, and salt in a heavy, 3-quart saucepan or pot with a lid. Bring to a boil, cover, and reduce the heat to low. Simmer for about 13 minutes, or until the water has evaporated and craters appear on the surface. Remove from the heat and fluff lightly with a fork to separate the grains. Cover, let sit for 5 minutes, then serve.

VARIATIONS: *Toast an additional ¼ cup unsweetened coconut in a frying pan over low heat until golden, stirring constantly. Let cool and sprinkle on top of the cooked rice before serving.*

For a heavier and more intense coconut flavor, substitute one 13.5-ounce can light coconut milk for 1½ cups of the water and prepare as directed.

> Coconut meat is warming and moisturizing to the body
> and a good source of saturated fat for vegetarians.

CURRY-FLAVORED WHOLE WHEAT COUSCOUS

4 TO 6 SERVINGS

While couscous does not traditionally accompany Asian dishes, I think it is very complementary. And it cooks in minutes. Whole wheat couscous has a pleasant nutty flavor and is found in most supermarkets. I like to dress it up a little, adding fresh herbs and other fragrant seasonings.

1½ tablespoons olive or canola oil

1 medium white onion, finely diced

1½ tablespoons minced garlic

1½ teaspoons Madras curry powder

2 cups whole wheat couscous

3 cups vegetarian broth or water

1 teaspoon salt

¼ teaspoon freshly ground black pepper

½ cup coarsely chopped cilantro leaves

2 tablespoons fresh lemon juice

1. Heat the oil in a medium saucepan with a lid over medium heat until very hot, about 20 seconds. Add the onion, garlic, and curry powder and stir-fry until the onion is soft and translucent, 4 to 5 minutes.

2. Add the couscous, broth or water, salt, and black pepper. Mix well and bring to a boil. Cover, reduce the heat to low, and simmer for 2 minutes, or until all the water has been absorbed. Remove from the heat and allow to stand for 5 minutes.

3. Fluff the cooked couscous with a fork and add the chopped cilantro and lemon juice. Taste for seasoning, adding more salt if necessary, and serve.

VARIATIONS: *Once the couscous is cooked, add 1½ cups cooked shelled edamame, 1½ cups peas, or a cooked vegetable of your choice that has been cut into bite-size pieces. Stir and add additional salt and pepper as needed.*

Substitute other seasonings for the curry powder, like dried basil, cumin, oregano, or another spice, and replace the chopped cilantro with fresh dill, basil, scallion greens, or flat or curly parsley.

FIVE-SPICE QUINOA
WITH TOASTED ALMONDS

4 TO 6 SERVINGS

Five-spice powder is a seasoning that usually includes star anise, cinnamon, licorice root, fennel, and black or Sichuan pepper. It plays well against the slight nuttiness of quinoa, a grain that is rich in protein. Toasting the quinoa in a little oil adds a pleasing nuance of flavor. If the quinoa is sold in bulk or loose, I recommend rinsing it. If it's in a package, you may omit this step.

2 cups quinoa

1½ tablespoons olive or canola oil

3 tablespoons minced scallions

1½ tablespoons minced fresh ginger

½ teaspoon five-spice powder

SAUCE (combine in a small bowl)

2¾ cups vegetarian broth

1½ tablespoons soy sauce

½ teaspoon toasted sesame oil

½ teaspoon salt

½ cup toasted sliced almonds

1. Rinse the quinoa, if necessary, in a bowl, using your hand as a rake, and drain in a sieve.

2. Heat the oil in a medium saucepan with a lid over medium-high heat until very hot, about 20 seconds. Add the scallions, ginger, and five-spice powder and stir-fry until fragrant, about 1 minute. Add the quinoa and stir-fry for 2 to 3 minutes. Add the Sauce and bring to a boil. Reduce the heat to low, cover, and cook for about 15 minutes, until the liquid is absorbed. The quinoa should be tender to the bite. Remove from the heat, uncover, and fluff with a fork.

3. If the almonds aren't toasted, cook them in a dry skillet over medium heat, stirring constantly, until golden brown. Let the quinoa cool slightly and then stir in the toasted almonds. Taste for seasoning, adding salt or soy sauce if necessary. Serve warm or at room temperature as a staple dish instead of rice or couscous.

> Not only is quinoa high in protein, but the protein it supplies is complete, meaning that it includes all nine essential amino acids. Quinoa is especially well-endowed with the amino acid lysine, which is essential for tissue growth and repair. In addition to protein, quinoa features a host of other health-building nutrients including magnesium, iron, copper, and phosphorus.

SPICY ORANGE FENNEL SLAW

4 SERVINGS

Fennel has become increasingly popular in the United States, but it is well known in Europe and the Mediterranean where the bulbs and fronds are used (both raw and cooked) in side dishes, salads, pastas, and vegetable dishes. Serve with Orange-Maple Salmon (page 91) or as a side dish.

2 fennel bulbs (about 1½ pounds)

3 large seedless oranges

SPICY ORANGE DRESSING (combine in a large bowl)

2 teaspoons chopped or grated orange zest (from one of the oranges above)

½ cup fresh orange juice

2 tablespoons minced fresh ginger

1 tablespoon extra-virgin olive oil

1 tablespoon Japanese rice vinegar

1 tablespoon chopped garlic

1½ teaspoons sugar

1 teaspoon ground cumin

1 teaspoon ground coriander

1¼ teaspoons salt

¼ teaspoon freshly ground black pepper

1. Trim the root end of the fennel bulbs and cut away the stalks and discard, reserving the fronds (leaves). Cut the fennel bulbs in half. Cut out the core and discard; cut the bulbs into very thin slices. Coarsely chop the fennel fronds and set aside.

2. Grate the zest and squeeze the juice of 1 orange; set aside. Peel the remaining 2 oranges and cut away the white pulp or pith. Separate the orange sections and cut each section crosswise in half. Mix the fennel and orange sections with the coarsely chopped fennel fronds in a serving bowl.

3. Taste the Spicy Orange Dressing for seasoning and adjust if necessary. Pour the dressing over the fennel and orange sections and toss lightly to coat. Cover and let sit or refrigerate to chill slightly.

SAKE-ROASTED BRUSSELS SPROUTS

4 TO 6 SERVINGS

I was never a huge fan of Brussels sprouts until I sampled some at a tapas bar that were tender-roasted. Their edges were crisp and caramelized. I experimented and came up with the easy, effortless recipe below.

2 pounds Brussels sprouts, rinsed and drained

2 tablespoons rice wine or sake, or dry white wine

2 teaspoons olive or canola oil

¾ teaspoon salt

¼ teaspoon freshly ground black pepper

1. Preheat the oven to 425°F and arrange a rack in the middle of the oven.

2. Using a sharp knife, trim the stem end of each Brussels sprout. Cut each sprout in half or, if large, into quarters. Toss lightly with the rice wine, oil, salt, and pepper. Arrange in a shallow 17×12-inch baking pan.

3. Cover with aluminum foil and roast for 20 minutes, or until the sprouts are just tender. Uncover and increase the oven temperature to 450°F. Toss lightly and continue roasting for 15 minutes, or until the edges are brown and crisp. Spoon the roasted sprouts into a serving bowl and serve as a side to Grilled Ginger Char (page 92) or another dish.

LEMONY EDAMAME

4 TO 6 SERVINGS

Edamame are soybeans, and they are usually sold frozen, either in their shells or shelled, in most Asian and mainstream supermarkets. Generally, I like to blanch the edamame (in their pods) briefly in boiling water, toss them in sea salt, and keep them on hand for snacking. I add shelled edamame to stir-fries, soups, salads, and curries, or serve as a simple side dish like this one.

1 bag (1 pound) frozen shelled edamame
   or soybeans

LEMON DRESSING (combine in a small bowl)

   3 tablespoons fruity extra-virgin olive oil

   2 tablespoons fresh lemon juice, or to
      taste

1 teaspoon salt

½ teaspoon freshly ground black
   pepper

1. Bring 6 cups water to a boil in a large pot. Drop the edamame into the boiling water, stir, and cook for 1 minute. Drain in a colander and rinse under cold running water. Drain thoroughly and place in a serving bowl.

2. Pour the Lemon Dressing over the edamame and toss lightly to coat. Serve at room temperature or chilled as a side dish with Scallion-Ginger Sea Bass (page 94) or another entrée.

> Edamame are not only rich in protein and fiber,
> but also believed to reduce the risk of heart disease.

SEARED BABY BOK CHOY

6 SERVINGS

Stir-frying is the quintessential Chinese technique for cooking all types of Chinese vegetables, especially greens. This recipe illustrates the basic steps. The key is to organize all the ingredients around the stove before you start cooking, and don't be afraid to get your pan really hot. The combination of oil, wine, and fire will give your vegetables that appealing wok-seared flavor.

1½ pounds baby bok choy

1 teaspoon olive or canola oil

2 tablespoons rice wine or sake, or very good quality dry sherry

1 tablespoon minced garlic

1 teaspoon sea salt, or to taste

1. Trim away the ends of the bok choy stalks and cut off and discard 1 inch of the leaf tips. Put the bok choy in the sink in water to cover and rinse thoroughly, since it is often sandy. Drain thoroughly. Cut the bok choy hearts in half along the length and, if very big, cut each half in half again.

2. Bring 3 quarts water to a boil. Add the bok choy and cook for about 2½ minutes, until crisp-tender. Drain and refresh in cold water. Drain thoroughly.

3. Heat the oil in a wok or a deep skillet over high heat until near smoking. (Don't be afraid to get the pan really hot. This gives the dish its special flavor.) Add the blanched bok choy, rice wine, garlic, and salt and toss lightly for about 1½ minutes, or until the bok choy is near tender but still bright green. Scoop out the vegetables, arrange on a serving platter, and spoon the pan juices on top. Serve immediately or at room temperature as a side dish to Teriyaki Halibut (page 95) or another entrée.

VARIATION: *Substitute any cruciferous vegetable (Chinese or Western) for the bok choy.*

GRILLED LEMON-SOY ZUCCHINI

4 TO 6 SERVINGS

Grilling vegetables may not be the traditional method favored in China, but the technique flash cooks and accentuates the flavor of food in a way similar to stir-frying.

5 medium zucchini (about 2 pounds), rinsed and drained

2 tablespoons olive or canola oil

1 teaspoon salt

1/4 teaspoon freshly ground black pepper

LEMON-SOY DRESSING (combine in a small bowl and stir until the sugar dissolves)

3 tablespoons soy sauce

2 tablespoons fresh lemon juice

1 1/2 tablespoons minced garlic

1 1/2 tablespoons sugar

1. Trim the ends of the zucchini and discard. Cut each lengthwise in half, then cut lengthwise in half again so you have four wedges of zucchini. Toss with the oil, salt, and pepper to coat.

2. Prepare a medium-hot fire for grilling or preheat a gas grill. Arrange a rack 3 to 4 inches from the heat. Arrange the zucchini on the grill rack (in batches if necessary) and grill for about 5 minutes on each side, until slightly golden at the edges and very tender. Test with the tip of a knife: It should pierce the zucchini easily. Remove and cut into 1/2-inch-wide pieces. Arrange on a serving platter.

3. Pour the Lemon-Soy Dressing over the zucchini. Serve warm, at room temperature, or cold as a side dish for grilled or roasted meats or seafood.

VARIATION: *Add 1 tablespoon dried herbs or 3 tablespoons chopped fresh herbs such as basil, dill, oregano, or tarragon to the dressing for additional flavor.*

MANGO SALSA

MAKES ABOUT 3 CUPS

There's something about the sweet and tangy flavor of fresh mango that complements grilled food beautifully. If mangoes aren't available, you can substitute peaches or pineapple.

4 ripe mangoes, about 1 pound each

1 small onion, minced

½ cup minced scallion greens

5 tablespoons fresh lime juice (from about 2 limes)

¼ cup chopped cilantro leaves

1 teaspoon curry powder

¼ teaspoon crushed red pepper flakes

1 teaspoon salt

¼ teaspoon freshly ground black pepper

One at a time, stand the mangoes upright on one of their pointed ends. Cut off the two fleshy cheeks on the sides, cutting as close to the pit as possible. Score or cut the flesh into ¼-inch dice. Scrape the flesh from the skin with a spoon into a serving bowl. Add the onion, scallion greens, lime juice, cilantro, curry powder, red pepper flakes, salt, and black pepper. Toss gently to mix and let sit briefly before serving.

Mangoes aid digestion and are an excellent source of beta-carotene and fiber. They may also help prevent cancer.

SWEET AND SOUR CUCUMBERS

6 SERVINGS

Due to its popularity, this sweet and sour pickle recipe appears, in some variation, in almost every book I've written. It can be made with carrots, daikon radishes, zucchini, and many other vegetables. The flavor intensifies with age, and the pickles are particularly delicious paired with grilled seafood and meats. I often add fresh or dried chili peppers for a little spiciness and color.

2 pounds English or pickling cucumbers, rinsed and drained

1 cup Japanese rice vinegar

1 cup sugar

1½ tablespoons minced fresh ginger

1 teaspoon salt

Trim the ends of the cucumbers. Slice lengthwise in half, scoop out any seeds with a spoon, and cut the cucumber on the diagonal into thin slices about ¼ inch thick. Put the slices in a bowl. Add the vinegar, sugar, ginger, and salt and toss lightly to coat. Cover with plastic wrap and let sit for 30 minutes or longer in the refrigerator. Serve cold.

VARIATION: *Add ¾ teaspoon crushed red pepper flakes or 1 teaspoon hot chili oil for extra flavor.*

ROASTED CHERRY TOMATO–CILANTRO SALSA

MAKES 3 CUPS

Some cooks overlook standard red cherry tomatoes, disdaining them for heirloom varieties. Admittedly, some can be bland in comparison to the other varieties, but roasting them truly brings out their sweet flavor.

1½ pounds or 2 pints cherry tomatoes

2½ tablespoons fruity extra-virgin olive oil

1½ tablespoons minced garlic

1 teaspoon salt

¼ teaspoon freshly ground black pepper

1 small jalapeño pepper

1 cup minced scallion greens

½ cup fresh cilantro leaves, chopped

2 tablespoons fresh lemon juice

1. Preheat the oven to 475°F. Rinse, drain, and blot the tomatoes dry with paper towels. Prick each tomato twice with the tip of a knife and place them in a bowl. Add the olive oil, garlic, salt, and pepper and toss lightly to coat. Arrange in a single layer in a nonaluminum pan and roast for 20 minutes; the tomatoes will be very tender.

2. Trim the ends of the pepper and discard with the seeds. Cut into little pieces and drop down the feed tube of a food processor fitted with a steel blade while the machine is running (or into a blender) and chop finely. Add the roasted tomatoes with their juice, the scallion greens, cilantro, and lemon juice. Taste and add more salt if necessary. Pour into a serving bowl and chill for 10 to 15 minutes before serving.

> Tomatoes contain an important phytonutrient, lycopene, that has been shown to prevent a number of forms of cancer, including prostate, colorectal, breast, endometrial, lung, and pancreatic.

ASIAN HOT AND SOUR SLAW

4 TO 6 SERVINGS

Some cooks may consider it cheating, but I have no qualms about using the shredded slaw mixes and shredded carrots in supermarket produce sections. They are particularly useful for preparing vegetable side dishes that complement all types of grilled and barbecued dishes.

1 tablespoon olive or canola oil

1/2 teaspoon sesame oil

2 tablespoons chopped fresh ginger

3/4 teaspoon crushed red pepper flakes

1 medium red pepper, cored, seeded, and diced

1 bag (14 or 16 ounces) shredded coleslaw

1 bag (10 ounces) shredded carrots

2 tablespoons rice wine or sake

HOT AND SOUR DRESSING (combine in a small bowl)

1/4 cup soy sauce

3 tablespoons sugar

2 tablespoons Chinese black vinegar or Worcestershire sauce

1/4 teaspoon salt

Heat the olive or canola oil and the sesame oil in a wok or a heavy skillet over medium-high heat until hot, but not smoking. Add the ginger and red pepper flakes and stir-fry until fragrant, about 10 seconds. Add the diced red pepper and toss lightly over high heat. Add the coleslaw and carrots and toss lightly. Add the rice wine, stir, and cover. Cook over medium-high heat for a minute or two. Uncover and add the Hot and Sour Dressing. Toss lightly for a minute and remove to a serving bowl. Serve hot, at room temperature, or cold.

SIMPLE RAITA

MAKES 3½ CUPS

Raita is a refreshing, yogurt-based condiment served with Indian meals to complement spicy dishes. I like to make a very simple homemade version with grated cucumbers and nonfat Greek yogurt seasoned with ground cumin and fresh cilantro.

1 English seedless cucumber (about ½ pound), rinsed and drained

2 cups plain nonfat Greek yogurt

2½ tablespoons coarsely chopped cilantro leaves

½ teaspoon ground cumin

1 teaspoon salt, or to taste

¼ teaspoon freshly ground black pepper

1. Trim the ends of the cucumber and discard. Slice lengthwise and scoop out any seeds with a spoon. Grate with a hand grater or the grating blade of a food processor. Using your hands, squeeze out any water.

2. Mix the grated cucumber, yogurt, cilantro, cumin, salt, and pepper in a bowl. Cover with plastic wrap and refrigerate for 10 minutes. Use as directed in the Tandoori Chicken Sliders recipe (page 102), or as a side to another main dish.

> Yogurt contains probiotics, which strengthen the digestive tract with good bacteria. It also contains calcium and vitamin D, so it helps to keep bones strong and prevent osteoporosis.

BALSAMIC-GINGER ROASTED SWEET POTATO FRIES

4 SERVINGS

My best friend Debby created the most irresistible and simple sweet potato fries. She cuts the potatoes by hand, but you can use the slicing attachment on a food processor or a mandolin to save time. Enjoy the roasted slices plain or with the reduced balsamic syrup.

4 tablespoons fruity extra-virgin olive oil

4 or 5 medium sweet potatoes (about 3$\frac{1}{4}$ pounds)

2 tablespoons minced fresh ginger

1 tablespoon salt

$\frac{1}{4}$ teaspoon freshly ground black pepper

1 cup balsamic vinegar (optional)

1. Preheat the oven to 425°F. Brush a baking sheet generously with 2 tablespoons of the oil. Peel the sweet potatoes and cut each in half lengthwise. With the cut side down, cut each half into $\frac{1}{2}$-inch-thick slices.

2. Mix the sweet potatoes in a bowl with the remaining 2 tablespoons oil, the ginger, salt, and pepper. Transfer to the prepared baking sheet and roast for 15 minutes, until crisp and golden brown. Remove with a spatula and let cool.

3. If using the balsamic vinegar, while the sweet potatoes are roasting, cook the vinegar in a heavy, nonreactive pan until reduced by half into a thick syrup. Serve the syrup as a dipping sauce on the side.

> Orange-fleshed sweet potatoes may be one of the most potent sources of beta-carotene and are thought to cleanse the digestive tract of harmful substances such as mercury. They contain a great deal of dietary fiber and, unlike many starchy vegetables, help regulate blood sugar.

CHUNKY AVOCADO SALSA

MAKES 5 TO 6 CUPS

This salsa is delicious, easy, and versatile. I serve it with many grilled foods, including seafood, pork, and chicken. It's also excellent as a dip with tortilla chips. To preserve the salsa and prevent it from darkening, bury the avocado pits in it, cover tightly, and store in the refrigerator.

¾ pound ripe tomatoes, rinsed and drained, stems removed

1 jalapeño pepper (or to taste), cored and seeded

2 avocados, peeled, pitted, and cut into ¼-inch dice

1 cup minced scallion greens

½ cup cilantro leaves, coarsely chopped

4½ tablespoons fresh lime juice (from 2 to 3 limes)

2 tablespoons fruity extra-virgin olive oil

1 tablespoon minced garlic

1 teaspoon salt

Cut the tomatoes in half and scoop out the seeds. Cut into ½-inch dice and put in a serving bowl. Mince the jalapeño pepper and add to the tomato, along with the avocado, scallion greens, cilantro, lime juice, olive oil, garlic, and salt. Carefully stir to mix evenly. Taste for seasoning and adjust if necessary.

Avocados may be high in calories, but their oil is a monounsaturated fat. They are also rich in potassium and antioxidants such as vitamins A, C, and E. Avocados also help lower cholesterol and regulate blood pressure, and are good for the skin.

SMOKY SESAME CORN ON THE COB

6 SERVINGS

Chris Schlesinger, owner of the East Coast Grill in Cambridge, Massachusetts, has inspired many of my grilled recipes through the years, including this one. In the masterful *Salsas, Sambals, Chutneys & Chowchows* (co-authored with John Willoughby), he uses grilled corn just as I do in this dish. Try it. It's easy, smoky, and delicious.

6 ears sweet corn

5 tablespoons fruity extra-virgin olive oil

½ teaspoon toasted sesame oil

1 tablespoon unsalted butter

4 large garlic cloves, finely chopped

Salt

Freshly ground black pepper

1. Break off the stem end of the corn ears and peel back the husks, but do not remove. Clean all the silk from around the ears and re-cover the exposed corn with the husks. Soak the corn in cold water for 10 minutes.

2. While the corn is soaking, heat 4 tablespoons of the olive oil, the sesame oil, and butter in a heavy saucepan until hot, about 350°F. Add the garlic, stir, and then turn off the heat. If the garlic begins to brown, remove the pan from the stove.

3. Prepare a hot fire for grilling or preheat a gas grill to 425°F. Arrange a rack 3 to 4 inches from the heat and brush or spray the rack with the remaining 1 tablespoon olive oil. Pile the coals to one side of the grill to create a cool section, or turn the heat on the gas grill to medium (about 350°F). Place the corn on the rack, still covered by the husks. Grill for about 5 minutes and, using tongs, turn the ears to the other side and grill for 5 minutes. Turn the corn again and grill for 4 more minutes, then remove from the heat. Peel the husks back and brush the corn with the seasoned oil. Serve with salt and pepper.

CORN AND PEPPER SALSA

MAKES 5½ CUPS

One of the best things about grilling corn is the delicious leftovers. Frankly, I'm very happy eating leftover grilled corn plain, but you can also make this simple salsa with roasted peppers. It is excellent paired with grilled or pan-seared seafood and meats.

6 ears Smoky Sesame Corn on the Cob
(page 141), or 4 cups frozen corn, defrosted

2 roasted red bell peppers from a jar, or whole
roasted peppers, skin and seeds removed,
blotted dry

3 scallions, ends trimmed

¼ cup unseasoned rice vinegar

2 tablespoons sugar

1 teaspoon toasted sesame oil

1 teaspoon salt

¼ teaspoon freshly ground black pepper

1. If using Smoky Sesame Corn on the Cob, hold the corn upright with the cut stem edge on the cutting board and cut down each ear with a sharp knife to remove the kernels. Cut the peppers into ½-inch dice. Finely chop the scallions.

2. In a serving bowl, combine the corn, red peppers, and scallions. Add the rice vinegar, sugar, toasted sesame oil, salt, and pepper. Mix, and season additionally to taste if necessary.

VARIATION: *Add one or two avocados cut into ½-inch dice. Add ¼ teaspoon salt and a pinch more ground black pepper to taste.*

PICKLED ONION, CORN, AND EDAMAME SALSA

MAKES 5 CUPS

For years I have made black bean salsa to accompany grilled dishes. At the suggestion of a friend, however, I substituted shelled edamame for the black beans, and the result was an equally delicious and colorful salsa. The edamame have a pleasingly crisp texture.

1 medium red onion, peeled, thinly sliced, and diced

1 tablespoon minced garlic

1/4 cup rice wine vinegar

3 ears sweet corn, husked, or 2 cups thawed corn kernels

1 red bell pepper, cored, seeded, and cut in 1/4-inch pieces

3 cups frozen shelled edamame (1 16-ounce package), defrosted

1 tablespoon minced fresh oregano, or 1 teaspoon dried

1 1/2 teaspoons Madras curry powder

1/2 teaspoon crushed red pepper flakes

4 heaping tablespoons chopped cilantro leaves

1 teaspoon salt

1/4 teaspoon freshly ground black pepper

1. Put the diced onion in a large bowl, add the garlic and vinegar, and mix. Cover with plastic wrap and set aside for 15 to 20 minutes.

2. Bring a large pot of water to a boil. Add the corn and cook for 10 minutes. Drain and rinse under cold running water until cool. Cut the corn from the cobs.

3. Add the corn to the bowl with onions, then add the remaining ingredients and combine. Taste for seasoning, adding additional salt if necessary. Cover with plastic wrap and chill briefly before serving. Serve with grilled or roasted seafood, meat, or chicken.

CHAPTER 6

ॐ

ASIAN STEWS
AND CASSEROLES

ASIAN STEWS AND CASSEROLES

LIKE WESTERN COOKS, Asians love meal-in-one casseroles for their convenience, versatility, and sumptuous flavors. What could be more welcoming than a kitchen suffused with the appetizing aroma of a bubbling pot of Garlic Sesame Chicken Smothered with Leeks or Lemongrass Shrimp Curry?

For the contemporary cook with a busy schedule, these dishes are a godsend. Assembling and prepping the various ingredients requires minimal effort, and then the stew can be left to cook in a slow cooker or over a low fire. A long, slow cook allows the flavors to mellow and blend, and the food can cook to a buttery tenderness. With seafood dishes, which may not require as much cooking time, the base can be prepared in advance, then briefly reheated and the seafood added at the last minute. Perhaps best of all, the following recipes taste even better the second time around, and many can be frozen and defrosted for future meals.

As noted above, many of these dishes can be prepared in Western slow cookers. The Chinese have their own version of slow cookers—unglazed clay pots similar to Romertopf and other European clay bakers. Traditional Chinese stoves were heated with wood or charcoal, and the top surface had round holes where clay cooking pots (and woks) were left to simmer unattended for hours.

Since I urge the cook to use whatever ingredients are on hand and available, feel free to substitute different seasonal vegetables and choose your staple of choice: rice, couscous, or a whole-grain pasta. Either way, these dishes are guaranteed to nurture, sustain, and provide infinite pleasure.

SPICY BRAISED HALIBUT WITH SWISS CHARD

4 TO 6 SERVINGS

My first inclination is to grill seafood, but in the cooler weather poaching or quickly braising a firm-fleshed fish fillet is equally delicious. I like to vary the dish by using whatever greens are available—from kale to Swiss chard.

1½ pounds halibut steaks or fillets, about ¾ inch thick, rinsed and patted dry

MARINADE (combine in a small bowl)

2 tablespoons rice wine or sake

1½ tablespoons minced ginger

1 bunch Swiss chard (about 1 pound)

SEASONINGS

3 scallions, ends trimmed

1½ tablespoons minced garlic

SAUCE (combine in a small bowl)

1½ cups chicken broth, preferably low-sodium

3 tablespoons soy sauce

1½ tablespoons sugar

1 tablespoon rice wine or sake

2 teaspoons Chinese black vinegar or Worcestershire sauce

2 teaspoons olive or canola oil

1 teaspoon toasted sesame oil

1 tablespoon cornstarch mixed with 2 tablespoons water

1. Place the fish in a bowl, add the Marinade, and toss lightly to coat. Set aside.

2. Rinse the Swiss chard and drain. Cut away the center ribs and stems and discard. Chop the leaves coarsely (about 5 cups). Mince the scallions (for the Seasonings) and set aside 2 tablespoons of the greens for garnish. Stir together the sauce ingredients.

3. Heat a Dutch oven or casserole dish with a lid over medium-high until very hot, about 30 seconds. Add the Seasonings and stir-fry for about 20 seconds, until fragrant. Add the Sauce and heat until boiling. Arrange the fish in the sauce, partially cover, and bring the liquid back to a boil. Reduce the heat to low and simmer for 5 to 6 minutes, until the fish is almost cooked. Add the Swiss chard and cook for 2 to 3 minutes, until the leaves are nearly tender and the fish flakes when prodded with a fork.

4. Remove the fish fillets with a slotted spoon and arrange in a shallow serving bowl. Slowly add the cornstarch mixture to the sauce in the pan, stirring constantly to prevent lumps, and cook until thickened. Pour over the fish, sprinkle with the reserved scallions, and serve.

VARIATION: *Substitute another firm-fleshed fish such as tilapia or red snapper for the halibut.*

LEMONGRASS SHRIMP CURRY

4 TO 6 SERVINGS

This vibrantly colored and flavored dish is a quick stew. I like to prepare the sauce in advance, precook the green beans, and then reheat all the ingredients together before serving. Paired with rice, couscous, or another grain, it can be served as a weeknight family meal or a festive dish for entertaining.

1 pound raw medium shrimp, peeled, deveined, rinsed, and drained

SEASONINGS

> 1 heaping teaspoon crushed red pepper flakes, or to taste
>
> 4 stalks lemongrass, or 2 tablespoons minced lemon zest
>
> 6 cloves garlic, smashed and peeled

1 pound green beans, ends snapped, cut in half diagonally

2 tablespoons olive or canola oil

1½ medium red onions, peeled, cut in half, and thinly sliced

1½ medium red peppers, cored, seeded, and thinly sliced (optional)

2 tablespoons rice wine or sake

COCONUT SAUCE (combine in a small bowl)

> 1 can (13.5 ounces) light coconut milk (1½ cups)
>
> 2½ tablespoons fish or soy sauce
>
> 1 tablespoon sugar
>
> 1½ teaspoons salt, or to taste

1 full cup shredded or torn fresh basil leaves

1. Rinse the shrimp in a colander and drain. Score the shrimp lengthwise along the back to butterfly, place in a bowl, and set aside.

2. Drop the Seasonings in listed order into a blender or the feed tube of a food processor while the machine is running and process to a rough, chopped mixture, turning the machine on and off several times.

3. Bring 2 cups water to a boil in a 3-quart casserole dish or a large skillet with a lid. Add the green beans and partially cook for about 4 minutes, until crisp-tender. Drain and refresh in cold water. Drain again.

4. Reheat the pan, add the oil, and heat over medium heat until hot. Add the Seasonings and cook, stirring with a wooden spoon, for about 1 minute, until fragrant. Add the red onions and stir-fry for about 1 minute. Add the red peppers (if using) and rice wine and toss lightly for 1 minute. Cover and cook for 2 to 3 minutes, until tender. Add the green beans and the Coconut Sauce. Increase the heat to medium-high and heat until boiling. Add the shrimp and simmer, covered, for about 2 minutes, or until the shrimp are cooked and the green beans are tender. Add the shredded basil and toss lightly. Spoon over steamed rice, whole wheat couscous, or another whole grain and serve.

VARIATIONS: *Substitute scallops, boneless, skinless chicken breast, or a thinly sliced firm-fleshed fish fillet for the shrimp.*

Substitute broccoli or snap or snow peas for the green beans. Precook broccoli about 3½ minutes and snow or snap peas for 1 minute. Refresh in cold water and drain.

In addition to its vibrant flavor, basil eases gas and helps
to strengthen the immune system.

EASY ASIAN SEAFOOD PAELLA

6 TO 8 SERVINGS

Like its Spanish cousin, this paella is brimming with seafood and spicy chorizo. The dish is a spectacular presentation and a meal-in-one feast.

1 pound skinless cod, red snapper, or other firm-fleshed fish fillets

1 pound sea or bay scallops, rinsed and drained

¾ cup rice wine or sake, or dry white wine

2 tablespoons minced ginger

12 ounces smoked Spanish chorizo

2 tablespoons olive or canola oil

1 large yellow onion, chopped

2½ tablespoons minced garlic

2 roasted red peppers from a jar, cut into ¼-inch dice

1½ cups raw white basmati rice

2 cups chicken broth, preferably low-sodium

1 can (14.5 ounces) diced tomatoes in juice

1½ teaspoons salt

1 teaspoon freshly ground black pepper

1 pound frozen shelled edamame or peas, defrosted

¼ cup coarsely chopped fresh cilantro (optional)

1. Cut the fish fillets into thin 1-inch squares, and cut the large scallops horizontally in half. In a bowl, mix the fish and scallops with the rice wine and ginger. Cut the chorizo on the diagonal into ¼-inch-thick slices.

2. Heat a large heavy skillet with a lid over medium-high heat. Add the chorizo and cook, stirring occasionally, for about 3 minutes, until the fat begins to render and the sausage slices become brown. Remove with a slotted spoon and drain on paper towels. Cut the chorizo into ½-inch dice.

3. Drain the fat from the skillet and discard. Reheat the skillet with the oil over medium heat until very hot, about 30 seconds. Add the onion and garlic and stir-fry until translucent, about 5 minutes. Add the cooked chorizo, red peppers, and rice and stir to coat. Drain the wine from the seafood into the pan, then scrape up the browned bits from the bottom of the pan. Add the chicken broth, tomatoes with juice, salt, and pepper. Bring the mixture to a simmer and cover the skillet tightly. Cook for about 12 minutes.

4. Add the fish and scallops and mix. Cover tightly again and cook for 5 to 7 minutes, until the seafood is cooked. Test the fish for doneness by cutting into a chunk; it should be flaky. Scatter the edamame over the top and sprinkle with the cilantro, if using. Cover and cook 1 minute more, then serve immediately.

LION'S HEAD CHICKEN WITH BABY BOK CHOY

6 SERVINGS

Lion's Head is a traditional slow-braised stew from eastern China made with ground pork meatballs and Napa cabbage. For my speedier version, which takes less than half the prep time, I sear ground chicken or turkey meatballs mixed with the fragrant seasonings and cook them briefly in chicken broth with baby bok choy. It's one of those intoxicatingly good mommy foods that tastes even better when reheated.

1 pound ground chicken

SEASONINGS

1½ tablespoons minced scallion greens

2 tablespoons minced fresh ginger

2½ tablespoons soy sauce

1 tablespoon rice wine or sake

1½ teaspoons toasted sesame oil

½ teaspoon freshly ground black pepper

1 tablespoon cornstarch

1 pound baby bok choy or Napa cabbage, rinsed and drained

2 tablespoons olive or canola oil

1½ tablespoons chopped garlic

½ cup rice wine or sake

2½ cups chicken broth, preferably low-sodium

1½ tablespoons soy sauce

¾ teaspoon salt, or to taste

1. Put the ground chicken and Seasonings in a bowl and mix to thoroughly combine. Dip your hands in water and shape the mixture into 6 plump ovals.

2. Trim the stem tips from the bok choy, cut an inch off the tips of the leaves, and discard. Cut lengthwise in half if large. Put the bok choy in the sink in water to cover and rinse thoroughly, since it is often sandy. Drain thoroughly. If using Napa cabbage, cut off the tough ends and discard. Cut lengthwise in half and cut the leaves into 2-inch squares. Separate the stem sections from the leafy ones.

3. Heat the oil in a Dutch oven or covered casserole dish over high heat until very hot, about 30 seconds. Slide the chicken balls into the pan, cover and sear on both sides until golden, 4 to 5 minutes. Lower the heat, cover, and cook for about 10 minutes. Remove the chicken balls from the pan and drain out a little of the oil.

(continued)

4. Add the baby bok choy (if using cabbage, add the stem sections), garlic, and rice wine and stir-fry over medium-high heat for 1 minute. Add the chicken broth, chicken balls, and leafy sections of the cabbage and bring to a boil. Reduce the heat to medium-low, partially cover, and simmer for about 15 minutes, until the cabbage is tender. Add the soy sauce and salt and skim the top to remove any impurities. Serve hot.

VARIATION: *Add 1 cup blanched and coarsely chopped water chestnuts to the chicken balls for additional crunch.*

Bok choy, and all members of the cruciferous family, contains phytonutrients that may lower the risk of cancer. It also contains vitamins A and C, and is an excellent source of fiber.

GARLIC-SESAME CHICKEN SMOTHERED WITH LEEKS

6 SERVINGS

This dish works beautifully in a slow cooker. Prepare through step 3, then transfer to a slow cooker and cook on high for 2½ hours.

1½ to 2 pounds bone-in skinless chicken legs and thighs

CHICKEN MARINADE (combine in a small bowl)

10 peeled garlic cloves, smashed

½ cup rice wine or sake

3 tablespoons soy sauce

1½ tablespoons toasted sesame oil

4 leeks (about 1½ pounds), ends trimmed

2 tablespoons olive or canola oil

½ cup chicken broth, preferably low-sodium

2 tablespoons fresh lemon juice

2 teaspoons salt

1 tablespoon cornstarch mixed with 3 tablespoons water

1. Rinse the chicken, drain, and pat dry. Place in a bowl, add the Chicken Marinade, and toss lightly to coat. Slice the leeks lengthwise through the white sections and rinse under cold running water to remove any dirt. Drain thoroughly and cut into 1½-inch lengths. Drain the chicken, reserving the marinade and the garlic cloves. Blot dry on paper towels.

2. Heat the oil in a large casserole dish or Dutch oven with a lid over medium-high heat until very hot. Arrange the chicken pieces, meat-side down, in the pan and sear until golden brown, 2 to 3 minutes. Remove the chicken with a slotted spoon.

3. Reheat the oil over medium-high heat until hot. Add the leeks and the garlic cloves from the marinade, cover, and cook for about 3 minutes, stirring occasionally. Add the reserved marinade, chicken broth, lemon juice, and salt. Bring to a boil, return the chicken to the pot, and bring to a boil again.

4. Reduce the heat, cover, and simmer until the chicken is cooked through, about 25 minutes.

5. Remove the chicken with a slotted spoon and arrange in a serving bowl. Skim the surface of the sauce, removing any fat or impurities. Increase the heat and add the cornstarch mixture, stirring to prevent lumps, and cook until thickened. Pour the sauce over the chicken and serve.

VARIATION: *Add 8 ounces of kale, cut into 1-inch squares, in step 3 and cook for 5 minutes.*

SPICY MA PO TOFU WITH EDAMAME

4 TO 6 SERVINGS

Ma Po Do Fu (or *Tofu*) is a classic Sichuanese dish packed with contrasting hot, sweet, sour, and salty flavors in each bite. I like to add a precooked vegetable such as shelled edamame or peas and serve it with steamed rice for an easy, delicious, and satisfying meal.

1 pound firm tofu, cut horizontally into 1-inch-thick slabs

3 teaspoons olive or canola oil

1 pound ground turkey, chicken, or pork

SEASONINGS

3 tablespoons minced scallions

2 tablespoons minced ginger

2 tablespoons minced garlic

½ teaspoon hot chili paste, or to taste

BRAISING MIXTURE (combine in a small bowl)

2 cups water

3 tablespoons soy sauce

2 tablespoons sugar

1½ tablespoons rice wine or sake

½ teaspoon five-spice powder (optional)

1 pound frozen shelled edamame, defrosted

2 tablespoons fresh lemon juice

1 tablespoon cornstarch mixed with 1½ tablespoons water

1. Wrap the slabs of tofu in paper towels and set a heavy weight, such as a heavy skillet, on top. Let stand for 15 minutes to remove excess water. Cut into ½-inch cubes.

2. Heat a large wok or skillet over high heat. Add 1 teaspoon of the oil and when hot, add the ground meat. Cook, using a spatula to break it up, until opaque throughout, 3 to 4 minutes. Transfer to a bowl. Add the Seasonings and stir-fry for 15 seconds, until fragrant. Add the Braising Mixture and bring to a boil. Add the tofu and ground meat and reduce the heat to low. Partially cover and cook for 20 minutes. Add the edamame and lemon juice, cover, and cook for about 1½ minutes, until the edamame is heated through. Slowly add the cornstarch mixture, stirring to prevent lumps, and cook until thickened. Spoon into a serving bowl and serve with steamed rice or a whole grain.

3. Add the remaining 2 teaspoons of oil to the wok and heat until hot.

WILD MUSHROOM AND CHICKEN CASSEROLE

6 TO 8 SERVINGS

Supermarkets now offer a wide variety of mushrooms, especially in the fall and winter. With just a few additional basic ingredients like chicken, onions, chicken broth, and spinach you can make a hearty, satisfying, and healthy meal-in-one pot.

¾ pound assorted wild mushrooms (such as shiitake, oyster, and cremini)

2 medium white onions, peeled

1½ tablespoons olive or canola oil

3½ pounds boneless, skinless chicken thighs

¾ cup chicken broth, preferably low-sodium

½ cup rice wine or sake

2 tablespoons soy sauce

½ teaspoon freshly ground black pepper

1 bag (6 ounces) baby spinach

1. Preheat the oven to 350°F. Cut away and discard the stems of the shiitakes. Trim the stems of the other mushrooms. Cut all the caps into thin slices. Cut the onions in half and cut into thin slices.

2. Heat 1 tablespoon of the oil in a large, heavy casserole dish with a lid over medium-high heat until hot, about 20 seconds. Arrange the chicken pieces in the pot and cook until golden brown, 4 to 5 minutes. Remove and set aside.

3. Reheat the casserole dish with the remaining ½ tablespoon of oil over medium-high heat until hot. Add the onions and stir for about 1½ minutes. Partially cover and cook until they become soft. Add the mushrooms and sauté for about 2 minutes. Partially cover and cook, stirring occasionally, until the liquid has evaporated and the mushrooms begin to brown, about 5 minutes.

4. Return the chicken pieces to the casserole along with the chicken broth, rice wine, soy sauce, and black pepper. Stir gently to mix and coat the chicken with the onion-mushroom mixture. Cover and bake for about 25 minutes, until the chicken is tender and cooked through. Add the spinach and stir. Cover and bake an additional 5 minutes. Remove and serve with rice or a whole grain.

VARIATION: *Substitute a cut-up whole chicken or bone-in chicken parts and increase the baking time to 45 minutes.*

Mushrooms like shiitake and maitake contain lentinan, a phytonutrient that strengthens the immune system.

JAPANESE PORK STEW WITH SCALLIONS

4 TO 6 SERVINGS

I first tasted this dish as a penniless student on my first visit to Japan years ago. It was February and temperatures were frigid, but I sustained myself with visits to the steamy communal baths and endless bowls of noodle soups and stews. This pork stew is still one of my favorite dishes over noodles or rice. I mix it up by adding different vegetables, but collard greens have become the popular choice in our household.

1½ pounds boneless pork loin or rump, trimmed of fat and gristle

12 scallions, ends trimmed

2 pounds collard greens

8 slices fresh ginger about the size of a quarter

2½ tablespoons olive or canola oil

RICH BRAISING LIQUID (combine in a small bowl)

2½ cups water

¾ cup rice wine or sake

½ cup soy sauce

3 tablespoons sugar

1. Cut the pork into 1-inch cubes. Cut the scallions into 1½-inch lengths and smash lightly with the flat edge of a knife. Discard the coarse stems and center ribs from the collard greens, then wash the leaves and drain. Cut the greens to 1½-inch lengths. Smash the ginger slices with the flat edge of a knife.

2. Heat 2 tablespoons of the oil in a large casserole dish or Dutch oven with a lid over high heat until very hot, about 30 seconds. Place the pork cubes in the bottom of the pan, as many as will fit, and sear, turning until golden brown all over. Remove with a slotted spoon. Reheat the oil and repeat with the remaining cubes.

3. Reheat the pan with the remaining ½ tablespoon oil until very hot, add the scallions and ginger, and stir-fry over medium-high heat for about a minute. Add the Rich Braising Liquid and bring to a boil.

4. Add the pork and reduce the heat to low. Simmer, partially covered, for 45 minutes, or until the pork is near tender. Skim off any fat or impurities from the broth. Add the collard greens and continue cooking for 15 to 20 minutes. Portion over whole wheat noodles or other grains and serve.

VARIATIONS: *Substitute Napa cabbage or bok choy for the collard greens. Trim and discard the stem ends of the leaves. Cut the leaves into 1½-inch squares. Add the stems in step 4 and cook for 2 minutes, then add the leafier sections and cook for another 2 minutes.*

PAN-SEARED PORK CHOPS WITH MULTI-COLORED PEPPERS

4 TO 6 SERVINGS

Pork chops are a thrifty and versatile cut of meat admirably suited for a weeknight dinner. I like to braise them with peppers, onions, a generous douse of oyster sauce, and a touch of chili paste for additional flavor.

6 bone-in pork chops (about 3½ pounds), trimmed of fat and gristle

3 tablespoons soy sauce

6 garlic cloves, smashed and peeled

2 medium onions, peeled

1 red bell pepper, cored and seeded

1 orange bell pepper, cored and seeded

2½ tablespoons olive or canola oil

2½ tablespoons minced fresh ginger

1 teaspoon hot chili paste (optional)

2 tablespoons rice wine or sake

BRAISING MIXTURE (combine in a small bowl)

2 cups chicken broth, preferably low-sodium

¼ cup rice wine or sake

5½ tablespoons oyster sauce

2 tablespoons fresh lemon juice

2 teaspoons sugar

½ pound snow or snap peas, ends snapped and veiny strings removed

1½ tablespoons cornstarch mixed with 3 tablespoons water

1. Place the pork chops in a bowl and add the soy sauce and smashed garlic. Rub the mixture over the surface of the pork chop and let sit. Cut the onions and red and orange peppers into thin julienne strips.

2. Heat 1½ tablespoons of the oil in a large casserole dish or Dutch oven with a lid over medium-high heat until very hot, about 30 seconds. Drain the pork chops, reserving the marinade. Cook the pork chops, in 2 batches if necessary, until golden brown, 2 or 3 minutes per side. Remove with a slotted spoon and drain.

3. Reheat the pan with the remaining 1 tablespoon oil over medium-high heat until hot, about 30 seconds. Add the onions, ginger, and chili paste, if using, and stir-fry for a few minutes. Add the reserved marinade and continue cooking for another minute. Add the red and orange peppers and the rice wine, partially cover, and cook for about 5 minutes, until tender. Add the Braising Mixture and reserved marinade, stir, and bring to a boil.

(continued)

4. Add the pork chops and reduce the heat to medium-low. Simmer, partially covered, for about 20 minutes, or until the chops are tender and cooked through.

5. Add the snow or snap peas to the pot. Stir, cover, and bring the liquid back to a boil. Slowly add the cornstarch mixture, stirring constantly to prevent lumps, and cook until thickened. Serve the pork chops and peppers with steamed rice, quinoa, or couscous.

VARIATIONS: *Substitute 3½ tablespoons chopped fermented, salted black beans for the oyster sauce, adding them with the chopped ginger, and prepare the recipe as directed.*

Use boned, skinless chicken thighs instead of the pork and prepare the recipe as directed.

TENDER BRAISED PORK WITH FENNEL AND SWEET POTATOES

6 TO 8 SERVINGS

Redolent with garlic, a hint of five-spice powder, and fennel, this pork is especially tender and is a succulent compliment to the fennel and sweet potatoes. You may substitute butternut or acorn squash for the sweet potatoes. Serve the stew atop a bed of rice, couscous or another whole grain.

2 pounds boneless pork butt or shoulder, trimmed of excess fat or gristle

1 teaspoon five-spice powder

6 garlic cloves, chopped finely or squeezed through a garlic press

½ teaspoon freshly ground black pepper

2 fennel bulbs (1½ pounds total) all but ½-inch of stalks and root base trimmed

2 sweet potatoes or yams, about 1½ pounds, peeled and cut into 1½-inch cubes

1½ tablespoons olive or canola oil

1 bunch scallions, ends trimmed, cut into 1½-inch sections, and smashed lightly with the flat side of a cleaver or knife

6 slices fresh ginger, about the size of a quarter, smashed lightly with the flat side of a cleaver or knife

BRAISING MIXTURE

4 cups water

Scant ½ cup soy sauce

¼ cup rice wine or sake

2 tablespoons sugar

2 tablespoons minced scallions for garnish (optional)

1. Cut the pork into 1½-inch cubes. Place in a bowl, add the five-spice powder, garlic, and black pepper. Toss lightly to coat and set aside. Cut each fennel bulb lengthwise in half. With the cut-side down, cut each half into slices ½-inch thick. Peel the sweet potatoes and cut into 1½-inch cubes.

2. Heat the oil until very hot in a 4-quart casserole or a Dutch oven. Add the scallion sections and ginger and stir-fry about 30 seconds until fragrant. Add the pork and continue stir-frying over medium-high heat for about 4 to 5 minutes until slightly golden.

3. Add the Braising Mixture, cover, and bring the liquid to a boil. Reduce the heat to low and simmer, covered, for 40 to 45 minutes. Add the fennel and sweet potatoes, stir, cover, and continue cooking for about 25 minutes or until the potatoes are tender. Skim the surface now and then to remove any fat or impurities. Sprinkle the top with the minced scallions, if using, and serve.

SUMPTUOUS BALSAMIC-GLAZED SHORT RIBS WITH GARLIC

4 TO 6 SERVINGS

What dish is more sumptuous or nurturing, especially in the cold weather, than braised short ribs? Inspired by Italian cooking authority Michele Scicolone and her book *The Italian Slow Cooker*, I created this easy and satisfying dish.

4 to 5 pounds bone-in beef short ribs

2 medium red onions, peeled

3 tablespoons olive or canola oil

3 tablespoons minced garlic

BRAISING MIXTURE (combine in a small bowl)

   3 cups chicken broth, preferably
   low-sodium

1 1/2 cups full-bodied red wine such as
   Cabernet Sauvignon

1/2 cup balsamic vinegar

1/4 cup soy sauce

3 tablespoons light brown sugar

1 pound frozen shelled edamame, defrosted
   to room temperature

1. Preheat the oven to 350°F. Trim the ribs of any excess fat. Cut the onions in half and then into julienne strips.

2. Heat the oil in a large casserole dish or Dutch oven with a lid over medium-high heat until very hot. Working in batches, cook the ribs until golden brown on both sides, about 10 minutes.

3. Drain all but 1 1/2 tablespoons of fat from the pot and reheat until very hot. Add the onions and garlic and stir-fry over medium-high heat for about 1 minute. Partially cover and cook until the onions are slightly transparent, 7 to 8 minutes. Add the Braising Mixture and the seared ribs and bring to a boil. Reduce the heat to medium-low and cook, uncovered, for 8 to 10 minutes.

4. Cover the pot and bake in the oven for about 2 hours, until the ribs are very tender. Using tongs, remove the ribs from the sauce and set aside. Skim the sauce to remove any fat and impurities. Place the pot on a burner, add the edamame, and cook the sauce until boiling. Add the ribs and serve with steamed rice or another whole grain.

VARIATION: *For the edamame, substitute other blanched or precooked vegetables cut into bite-size pieces, such as broccoli, baby bok choy, snow or snap peas, or carrots.*

ANISE-FLAVORED BEEF STEW WITH RED WINE AND ORANGE PEEL

6 TO 8 SERVINGS

Star anise, with a pungent licorice-like flavor, is a wonderful complement to beef and red wine, and adds another dimension of flavor to this dish. Use it carefully, however, as it can easily overpower. Serve this dish over a crisp-cooked green vegetable or slices of fennel with steamed rice.

2 pounds beef stewing meat, such as chuck or bottom round, trimmed of fat and gristle

½ cup all-purpose flour

2 teaspoons salt

½ teaspoon freshly ground black pepper

Peel from 1 orange

6 small onions (about 1 pound), peeled

1 pound baby carrots or large carrots

3 tablespoons olive or canola oil

8 cloves garlic, smashed and peeled

1½ whole star anise, smashed

2 cups red wine, such as Cabernet Sauvignon

½ cup rice wine or sake

½ cup chicken broth, preferably low-sodium

1. Preheat the oven to 350°F. Cut the meat into 1½-inch cubes. On a plate or in a paper bag, mix the flour, salt, and pepper. Coat the meat with the seasoned flour, either by rolling the pieces on the plate or dropping into the bag and shaking. Lightly squeeze the meat pieces to adhere the flour to the surface. Discard the excess flour.

2. Bring 2 quarts of water to a boil, add the orange peel, and boil for 1 minute. Drain, blot on paper towels, and cut into thin julienne strips. Cut each peeled onion into 6 wedges. If using large carrots, peel and cut in half lengthwise, then cut into 1½-inch lengths.

> According to Chinese doctors, beef is considered
> very yang and is often consumed in the cold weather
> to counterbalance the yin conditions.

3. Heat 1½ tablespoons of the oil in a 4-quart casserole dish or a Dutch oven over medium heat until very hot. Add a batch of the beef and brown on all sides. Remove with a slotted spoon. Heat the remaining oil and brown the remaining beef.

4. Remove all but 1 tablespoon of the oil from the pot and add the onion wedges, garlic, and star anise. Cook over medium-high heat until fragrant, about 30 seconds. Add the red wine, rice wine, and chicken broth and stir to mix. Add the beef cubes and carrots and bring to a boil.

5. Cover tightly and bake in the middle of the oven, stirring occasionally, for about 1½ hours, until the beef and vegetables are very tender. Taste for seasoning, adding more salt if necessary, and skim any fat or impurities from the surface. Serve with rice or another whole grain.

Star anise has been used by Chinese and Ayurvedic doctors
for centuries. It is soothing to the stomach and used
as a breath freshener and in cough medications. The oil from
star anise is believed to relieve rheumatism.

CHAPTER 7

৪৩৫৫

SUMPTUOUS VEGETARIAN FARE

SUMPTUOUS VEGETARIAN FARE

NOT LONG AGO, the mere mention of vegetarian food would elicit a yawn or a groan, but not anymore. Just check out the wide selection of tofu and vegetarian products in supermarkets. It's really inspirational, and one of the reasons that so many of these foods have become essential ingredients in my everyday repertoire of dinner dishes.

I became a vegetarian enthusiast many years ago in Asia. Prior to that, in the seventies, I briefly cooked at a vegetarian restaurant during my one year of college. Overall, the dishes were brown, bland, and boring.

In Asia, it was just the opposite. The vegetarian foods I tasted were vibrantly flavored, colorful, and eclectic. I will never forget a banquet I enjoyed in a Buddhist temple in Taiwan at the very beginning of my stay there. Each meatless—but sumptuous—course was more enticing than the last. Dishes were beautifully seasoned with pungent flavorings like garlic, ginger, and toasted sesame oil and embellished with fresh herbs. Sauces resonated with a symphony of flavors. I was hooked and intrigued.

Ironically, as the West has embraced a fascination and grown an appetite for vegetarian foods, many countries in Asia, particularly China, have gone in the opposite direction, adding more meat and animal protein to their diets. The result has been an alarming increase in the "diseases of prosperity," namely, heart disease, hypertension, type 2 diabetes, and various types of cancer. It is a phenomenon that has led to spiraling increases in health costs and concern among public health officials.

If you aren't already a vegetarian enthusiast, I challenge you to try some of the dishes in this chapter and see if you find them lacking. Why not introduce yourself to a totally satisfying and enjoyable way of eating? You might be surprised, and I guarantee that even hard-core carnivores will not be disappointed.

RAINBOW OMELETS WITH SPICY KUNG PAO SAUCE

4 TO 6 SERVINGS

I like to prepare this dish for an easy weeknight dinner or a weekend brunch. I vary the vegetables depending on what's in season and available in my refrigerator.

2 tablespoons olive or canola oil

1 medium yellow or orange bell pepper, cored, seeded, and cut into thin julienne strips

1 small red onion, halved and thinly sliced

¼ pound snow or snap peas, ends snapped and veiny strings removed, halved

8 large eggs, lightly beaten

KUNG PAO SEASONINGS

2 tablespoons minced ginger

1½ tablespoons minced garlic

1 teaspoon hot chili paste with garlic, or crushed red pepper flakes

SAUCE (combine in a small bowl)

1¼ cups water

5 tablespoons soy sauce

3½ tablespoons rice wine or sake

2 tablespoons sugar

1½ tablespoons Chinese black vinegar or Worcestershire sauce

1⅓ tablespoons cornstarch

1. Heat 1½ tablespoons of the oil in a large nonstick skillet over high heat until very hot, about 20 seconds. Add the pepper, onion, and snow or snap peas and stir-fry for about 1½ minutes, until crisp-tender. Pour the eggs into the pan and tilt the pan so that the eggs form an even omelet. Cook over medium heat for 2 minutes, or until golden brown on the bottom. Reduce the heat to low, cover, and cook until set, 5 to 6 minutes. Using a knife, cut the omelet in half and flip each half over with a spatula. Cook for 2 minutes more, then scoop onto a cutting board.

2. While the omelet is cooking, heat the remaining ½ tablespoon oil in a medium saucepan or skillet over high heat until very hot, about 20 seconds. Add the Kung Pao Seasonings and stir-fry until fragrant, about 15 seconds. Add the Sauce and cook, stirring continuously to prevent lumps, until thickened.

3. Cut each half of the omelet into 3 or 4 wedges. Arrange on a deep serving dish and pour the spicy sauce on top, or pour the sauce into a bowl and serve on the side.

GOLDEN TEMPEH-NOODLE SALAD
WITH SPICY PEANUT SAUCE

6 SERVINGS

Tempeh, which is made from fermented soybeans, has a distinctively nutty taste and a slightly chewy texture. It is particularly high in protein, which makes it an excellent substitute for meat. It is usually found in the produce section of the market next to tofu. Pan-frying the tempeh gives it a crisp texture and appealing flavor.

1 package (8 ounces) multi-grain tempeh

1 1/2 tablespoons soy sauce

1 tablespoon rice wine or sake

1 teaspoon chopped garlic

1 medium red bell pepper, cored and seeded

1 medium orange or yellow bell pepper, cored and seeded

8 ounces whole wheat spaghetti

1 1/2 teaspoons toasted sesame oil

1 package (10 ounces) shredded carrots (about 4 cups)

1 package (9 ounces) broccoli slaw (about 3 1/2 cups)

3 tablespoons olive or canola oil

SPICY PEANUT SAUCE

2 1/2-inch knob of peeled ginger, cut into 1/4-inch slices (about 2 tablespoons)

5 cloves garlic, smashed and peeled

3/4 cup smooth peanut butter

1/4 cup soy sauce, or to taste

5 to 6 tablespoons vegetarian broth or water

3 1/2 tablespoons sugar

3 1/2 tablespoons Chinese black vinegar or Worcestershire sauce, or to taste

3 1/2 tablespoons toasted sesame oil

1 teaspoon hot chili paste, or to taste

1. Cut the tempeh horizontally in half and place in a bowl. Add the soy sauce, rice wine, and chopped garlic. Rub the marinade all over the tempeh and let sit. Cut the peppers into 1/4-inch-thick slices.

2. Bring 3 quarts of water to a boil in a large pot. Add the whole wheat noodles and cook for a little less time than directed on the package instructions. Drain in a colander and rinse thoroughly under warm water. Drain again and toss lightly with the sesame oil. Put the noodles in a large, deep serving dish. Arrange the pepper slices, shredded carrots, and broccoli slaw in separate concentric circles on top of the noodles, leaving room in the center for the tempeh. Reserve a few slices of the red pepper.

3. Heat the oil in a large skillet over medium-high heat until hot, about 20 seconds. Fry the tempeh halves on both sides until golden brown, about 5 minutes. Remove and drain on paper towels. Using a sharp or serrated knife, cut into ¼-inch-thick slices. Arrange the tempeh in the center of the salad and scatter the reserved red pepper slices on top.

4. To make the Spicy Peanut Sauce: In a food processor, or in a blender fitted with a steel blade, drop the ginger slices and garlic through the feeder tube while the machine is running. Add the remaining sauce ingredients and process until smooth. Taste and add more soy sauce, black vinegar, or chili paste if necessary. Pour the sauce into a serving bowl and serve on the side.

VARIATION: *Substitute very firm tofu for the tempeh.*

BEST-EVER VEGETARIAN FRIED RICE

6 SERVINGS

Rice is a pleasing staple that can be garnished with any leftover meat, seafood, or vegetables. This enticing vegetarian version is excellent as a light meal by itself or served with a stir-fried, steamed, or grilled meat or seafood. I use teriyaki-flavored baked tofu here; use any flavor you prefer.

1 package (8 ounces) teriyaki-flavored baked tofu

5 scallions, ends trimmed

3 tablespoons olive or canola oil

1 cup grated or shredded carrots

3 large eggs, lightly beaten

1/2 pound frozen shelled edamame, defrosted to room temperature

4 cups cooked long-grain white or brown rice, chilled and fluffed with a fork

SAUCE (combine in a small bowl)

3 tablespoons rice wine or sake

2 1/2 tablespoons soy sauce

1 teaspoon toasted sesame oil

1/2 teaspoon salt

1/4 teaspoon freshly ground black pepper

1. Cut the tofu into 1/4-inch dice. Mince the white sections of the scallions and cut the greens into 1/2-inch sections.

2. Heat the oil in a wok or heavy skillet over high heat until very hot, about 20 seconds. Add the scallions (both white and green) and carrots and stir-fry for about 1 minute. Add the eggs and stir-fry to scramble, turning up the heat to high. Push the food over to the side of the pan or remove to allow the pan to get really hot.

3. Once the eggs are cooked and the pan is really hot, add the diced tofu and edamame and toss lightly to heat through, about 2 minutes. Add the rice, using a spatula to mash and separate the grains. Cook for 3 to 4 minutes, until heated through and until some of the ingredients are lightly golden. Add the Sauce and toss lightly to coat. Taste for seasoning, adding any additional salt if necessary. Spoon the fried rice into a serving dish and serve.

VARIATIONS: *Substitute 1 pound diced cooked pork, chicken, beef, or shrimp for the tofu.*

Add 1/4 cup coarsely chopped cilantro or flat or leafy parsley for additional flavor.

GARLICKY STUFFED BLACK BEAN SQUASH

4 SERVINGS

Even meat lovers and tofu skeptics will be satisfied with this hearty and savory vegetarian dish. Black bean sauce, redolent of garlic and ginger, blankets stuffed squash in a velvety richness. I like to use delicata, sweet dumpling, or acorn squash, all of which have a firm, almost meaty texture.

1 square (about 1 pound) very firm tofu,
    cut horizontally into 1-inch-thick slabs

1 leek (about 3/4 pound), split lengthwise

2 medium delicata or acorn squash
    (2 1/2 to 3 pounds)

2 tablespoons olive or canola oil

SEASONINGS

1/4 cup prepared black bean garlic sauce

3 tablespoons minced garlic

2 tablespoons minced fresh ginger

1 teaspoon garlic chili paste

2 tablespoons rice wine or sake

SAUCE (combine in a small bowl)

1 1/2 cups water

3 tablespoons rice wine or sake

2 1/2 tablespoons soy sauce

2 1/2 teaspoons sugar

2 teaspoons cornstarch

1 teaspoon toasted sesame oil

1. Preheat the oven to 375°F. Line a baking pan with aluminum foil.

2. Wrap the slabs of tofu in paper towels and set a heavy weight, such as a heavy skillet, on top. Let stand for 15 minutes to remove excess water. Cut into 1/4-inch cubes. Trim the root end and the first few inches of green section of the leek and discard. Rinse the leek thoroughly under cold running water. Cut the leek into 1 1/2-inch lengths and then into julienne slices. Reserve 1 tablespoon of the leek green for the garnish.

3. Rinse the squash and pat dry. With a sharp knife or cleaver, cut each squash in half crosswise. With a melon baller or sharp knife, scoop out the seeds and some of the pulp to create a deep cavity. Arrange the squash, cut side up, on the prepared pan and pour 1/2 cup of water around it.

(continued)

4. To make the black bean filling, heat the oil in a heavy skillet over medium-high heat until very hot, about 20 seconds. Add the julienned leek and the Seasonings and stir-fry for about 15 seconds, until very fragrant. Add the rice wine and cook for about 1½ minutes, until the leeks are tender. Add the cubed tofu and the Sauce and bring to a boil. Cook, stirring slowly and constantly to prevent lumps, until the sauce thickens.

5. Spoon the filling generously into the cavities of the squash. (If there is extra filling, put in a small, greased ramekin, cover with parchment paper, and bake on the side.) Lightly brush the surface of a piece of aluminum foil with the toasted sesame oil and cover the squash with it, oiled surface down. Bake the squash in the middle of the oven for 35 to 40 minutes, until tender. Test with a knife, piercing into the center; the knife should come out easily. (The baking time will vary depending on the size of the squash. Medium delicata or acorn squash will take about 35 minutes, while larger acorn squash may take 45 to 55 minutes.) Sprinkle the tops with the reserved leek greens and serve with rice or another whole grain.

> Winter squash is warming to the body, improves *qi* and circulation, contains natural sugars, and is rich in vitamin A.

GRILLED TERIYAKI VEGETABLE SKEWERS

4 TO 6 SERVINGS

This vibrantly flavored teriyaki sauce is easy to prepare and delicious with vegetables, tofu, meat, and seafood. I like to make a large batch and refrigerate it so I can quickly put together an appealing and flavorful dish such as the one below. Serve with plain rice or one of the flavored rice dishes on pages 112 to 120.

1 square (about 1 pound) very firm tofu, cut horizontally into 1-inch-thick slabs

TERIYAKI SAUCE

$\frac{1}{3}$ cup soy sauce

$\frac{1}{3}$ cup rice wine or sake

$\frac{1}{3}$ cup water

7 tablespoons sugar

$1\frac{1}{2}$ tablespoons minced fresh ginger

1 teaspoon crushed red pepper flakes

$1\frac{1}{2}$ tablespoons cornstarch

1 medium red onion, peeled

2 red or orange bell peppers, cored and seeded

$\frac{1}{2}$ pound cremini mushrooms

10-inch bamboo skewers (6), soaked in water to cover for 10 minutes

2 tablespoons olive or canola oil, or olive oil spray, for oiling the grill

1. Wrap the slabs of tofu in paper towels and set a heavy weight, such as a heavy skillet, on top. Let stand for 15 minutes to remove excess water. Cut the tofu into 1-inch cubes.

2. While the tofu is sitting, make the Teriyaki Sauce: Mix all the ingredients in a heavy, medium saucepan over medium heat and cook until thickened, stirring constantly with a wooden spoon to prevent lumps. Remove and cool slightly.

3. Cut the onion in half, and then cut each half in half again. Separate the pieces. Cut the peppers into 1-inch squares. Trim the stems of the cremini mushrooms.

4. Alternately thread the skewers with the onion pieces, peppers, mushrooms, and tofu, starting and ending with onion. Place on a deep platter or a rimmed baking sheet lined with aluminum foil. Pour the teriyaki sauce over the skewers and turn so that the food is coated with the sauce. Let sit for 10 to 15 minutes.

(continued)

5. Prepare a medium-hot fire for grilling or preheat a gas grill. Arrange a rack 3 to 4 inches from the heat. Brush or spray the grill rack with oil. Arrange the skewered vegetables and tofu on the grill. Pour the remaining sauce into a small pan and reheat until hot.

6. Grill the vegetables, covered, for about 8 minutes on each side, or until the tofu edges are a deep golden color and the peppers are tender. Arrange the skewers on a serving platter. Pour the heated teriyaki sauce on top. Serve with rice or another whole grain.

VARIATIONS: *Bake the vegetables and tofu in a 425°F oven for 10 to 15 minutes, until the edges are slightly golden. Serve with the reheated teriyaki sauce on the side in a saucer or pour on top.*

Replace the tofu with 1 pound of raw shelled shrimp or 1½-inch cubes of skinned chicken breast, pork tenderloin, or beef tenderloin. Grill over a medium-hot fire, turning once, for 4 to 5 minutes for the shrimp or 6 to 7 minutes for the chicken and beef.

> Tofu, which is made from soybeans, is an excellent source
> of vegetable protein. It may help reduce heart disease,
> and it contains phytoestrogens, which help strengthen bones
> and prevent osteoporosis.

SAUCY LO MEIN NOODLES
WITH TRI-COLORED VEGETABLES

6 SERVINGS

This is one of my family's favorite meals (although my son Jesse tends to like his with shreds of barbecued pork). You can make the dish either with linguine or fettuccine. The wider noodle is a lovely foil for the rich sauce.

9 ounces linguine or fettuccine noodles

3 leeks or 1 bunch garlic chives

2 tablespoons olive or canola oil

3 tablespoons minced fresh ginger

2 1/2 tablespoons minced garlic

2 cups grated carrots (half of a 10-ounce bag)

1 bag (12 ounces) shredded broccoli slaw (4 1/2 cups)

2 tablespoons rice wine or sake

SAUCE (combine in a small bowl)

2 1/4 cups vegetarian broth or water

7 tablespoons oyster sauce

3 tablespoons soy sauce

3 tablespoons rice wine or sake

1 1/2 teaspoons toasted sesame oil

1 teaspoon sugar

1/4 teaspoon freshly ground black pepper

1 1/2 tablespoons cornstarch

1. Heat 4 quarts water until boiling, add the noodles, and cook until al dente, 2 1/2 to 4 minutes for fresh noodles or 7 to 9 minutes for dried. Drain in a colander, rinse lightly to remove the starch, and drain again thoroughly.

2. Thoroughly rinse the leeks or garlic chives under cold running water and drain thoroughly. Cut the leeks lengthwise into julienne slices. (Leave the chives in 1 1/2-inch lengths.)

3. Heat the oil in a deep skillet or frying pan over medium-high heat until very hot, about 20 seconds. Add the ginger and garlic and stir-fry for about 10 seconds, until fragrant. Add the leeks or garlic chives, the carrots, and broccoli slaw and stir-fry for about 1 1/2 minutes. Add the rice wine, lower the heat slightly, and cover. Cook, stirring occasionally, until just tender, about 3 minutes. Add the Sauce, increase the heat to high, and cook, stirring continuously to prevent lumps, until thickened. Add the cooked noodles and toss together until hot. Spoon the lo mein onto a warm platter and serve.

VARIATION: *Add additional vegetables, such as 2 cups of bean sprouts, or substitute 1 bunch kale, tough ribs discarded, rinsed, drained, and the leaves cut into julienne slices, for the broccoli slaw.*

CURRIED COCONUT STEW WITH FRESH HERBS

6 SERVINGS

These days, cooking a vegetable stew is almost effortless thanks to the prepared products sold in supermarkets: Green beans are presnapped, squash is peeled and precut. This intoxicatingly sumptuous dish is a great meal, especially in cooler weather.

1 square (about 1 pound) extra-firm tofu, cut horizontally into 1-inch-thick slabs

2 medium red onions, peeled

1¼ pounds butternut squash, peeled and seeded, or one 20-ounce package precut squash

½ pound (or one 12-ounce bag) trimmed green beans

CURRY SEASONINGS

2 slices peeled fresh ginger about the size of a quarter

1½ teaspoons ground cumin

1½ teaspoons ground coriander

1 teaspoon crushed red pepper flakes

1 teaspoon salt

½ teaspoon freshly ground black pepper

1½ tablespoons virgin olive oil

SAUCE (combine in a small bowl)

1½ cans (13.5 ounces each) light unsweetened coconut milk (3 cups)

3 tablespoons fish sauce

1½ tablespoons sugar

1 pound baby carrots

½ cup shredded fresh basil leaves

1. Wrap the slabs of tofu in paper towels and set a heavy weight, such as a heavy skillet, on top. Let stand for 15 minutes to remove excess water. Cut into 1-inch cubes. Cut the onions into small dice. Cut the butternut squash into 1½-inch squares. Cut the green beans in half on the diagonal.

2. Drop the Curry Seasonings into the feed tube of a food processor fitted with a metal blade while the machine is running. Turn the machine on and off to chop the seasonings evenly and mince to a coarse powder.

(continued)

3. Heat the oil in a heavy casserole dish or Dutch oven over medium-low heat until very hot, about 20 seconds. Add the curry seasonings and diced onions and cook, partially covered and stirring with a wooden spoon, for about 3 minutes, until the onions are tender and the seasonings are fragrant. Add the Sauce and bring to a boil. Add the tofu, squash, and carrots and stir to coat the vegetables with the sauce. Bring the mixture back to a boil and reduce the heat to low. Cover and cook for 15 to 20 minutes, until the squash is al dente.

4. Add the green beans and stir. Continue to cook for 5 to 7 minutes, until the green beans are tender. Scoop into a serving dish or serve from the casserole. Sprinkle in the fresh basil and toss lightly for a few seconds to coat. Serve with rice or another whole grain.

VARIATION: *Substitute fresh parsley or cilantro for the basil.*

> Soy foods such as tofu are a rich source of protein, can lower cholesterol, and may help prevent certain types of cancer.

STIR-FRIED MEATY PORTOBELLO MUSHROOMS WITH SOBA

6 SERVINGS

Nutty soba noodles are an excellent staple for an eclectic variety of stir-fries. Add cooked meat, seafood, or tofu and other vegetables like broccoli for a quick, healthy, and delicious dinner.

8 ounces soba noodles

3 tablespoons olive or canola oil

SEASONINGS

1 medium red onion, cut into 1/4-inch dice

2 tablespoons chopped garlic

1 package (6 ounces) sliced portobello mushrooms, or 10 whole portobello mushrooms, stems trimmed, sliced

8 ounces sliced baby bella mushrooms

2 tablespoons rice wine or sake, or dry white wine

SAUCE (combine in a small bowl)

2 tablespoons soy sauce

1 tablespoon balsamic vinegar

1/4 cup coarsely chopped cilantro leaves

1. Bring 3 quarts of water to a boil in a large pot and add the soba noodles. Once the water reaches a boil, reduce the heat slightly and cook for 3 1/2 minutes, until al dente. Drain in a colander and rinse the noodles under warm running water. Drain again.

2. Heat the oil in a large, heavy skillet or wok over medium-high heat until very hot, about 20 seconds. Add the Seasonings and stir-fry until very fragrant, about a minute. Add the mushrooms and stir-fry for about a minute. Add the rice wine, toss lightly, and cover. Cook for about 2 minutes, until the mushrooms are tender and have rendered liquid.

3. If the soba have stuck together, rinse briefly and drain thoroughly. Turn the heat to high and add the soba and the Sauce to the mushrooms. Stir-fry lightly until heated through and mixed well, about 2 minutes. Add the chopped cilantro and toss again to mix. Scoop out onto a serving platter and serve hot or at room temperature.

> Soba noodles, which are made with buckwheat flour and wheat flour, are believed to cleanse and energize the body.

FIVE-TREASURE SOUP POT

6 TO 8 SERVINGS

For Sunday lunch, my Chinese mother and I often made a large pot of soup filled with many different "treasures." These could range from seasonal vegetables to a fish head. This sumptuous soup will last for several meals.

10 dried Chinese black mushrooms

1 medium-size head Chinese Napa cabbage (about 1½ pounds)

1 pound firm tofu, cut horizontally into 1-inch-thick layers

2 teaspoons olive or canola oil

MINCED SEASONINGS

3 tablespoons minced fresh ginger

3 tablespoons minced garlic

1 bunch scallions (6 to 8), ends trimmed

1 cup rice wine or sake

SOUP SEASONINGS

4½ tablespoons soy sauce, or to taste

½ teaspoon freshly ground black pepper

¾ teaspoon salt, or to taste

1 teaspoon toasted sesame oil

½ pound baby carrots

1½ ounces cellophane noodles, softened in hot water to cover for 15 minutes and drained

1. Place the black mushrooms in a bowl and add 3 cups hot water. Soften for 15 minutes, then drain, reserving the liquid. Remove and discard the stems and cut the caps into 3 or 4 slices, depending on their size.

2. Cut away the stem of the cabbage and discard. Cut the cabbage in half and cut the leaves into 1½-inch squares, separating the leafy sections from the thicker center pieces.

3. Wrap the slabs of tofu in paper towels and set a heavy weight, such as a heavy skillet, on top and let stand 15 minutes to remove excess water. Cut the tofu into ½-inch cubes. Mince the white sections of the scallions and add to the seasonings. Cut the scallion greens diagonally into ½-inch lengths and set aside.

4. Heat a Dutch oven or a covered casserole, add the oil and heat until very hot, about 30 seconds. Add the Minced Seasonings and stir-fry over medium-high heat until fragrant, 20 seconds. Add the center sections of the cabbage and stir-fry for 1 minute. Add the rice wine and toss lightly; cover the pot and cook for 1½ minutes. Uncover the pot, add the remaining cabbage sections, the mushroom soaking liquid, and 4 cups of water. Cover and bring the liquid to a boil, reduce the heat slightly, and simmer for 30 minutes. Add the Soup Seasonings and stir.

5. Arrange the black mushrooms, tofu, carrots, and cellophane noodles on top of the cabbage in individual piles. Cover the pot again and continue cooking over medium-low heat for 20 minutes. Sprinkle with the scallions and taste for seasonings, adding a little more salt if necessary. Serve hot.

VARIATION: *Use teriyaki- or Thai-flavored tofu instead of plain tofu.*

Replace the soy sauce and salt with about ½ cup sweet white miso (miso shiro). *Mix with ½ cup of the broth before adding.*

Chinese doctors believe that cabbage improves digestion and eases constipation. It also is a rich source of vitamins A and C.

MU SHU VEGETABLES WITH STEAMED PANCAKES

4 TO 6 SERVINGS

Mu shu has become a staple of American-Chinese cuisine and is the quintessential stir-fry. There are numerous variations made with pork, chicken, or shrimp, but my favorite is vegetarian, redolent with scallions, various mushrooms, and cabbage. I like to take advantage of every shortcut, using a shredded coleslaw mix and frozen or takeout Mandarin pancakes.

4 ounces shiitake mushrooms

6 ounces cremini mushrooms

2 tablespoons olive or canola oil

2 large eggs, lightly beaten

1 teaspoon salt

SEASONINGS (combine in a small bowl)

$\frac{1}{4}$ cup minced scallions, white sections only

3 tablespoons minced garlic

3 tablespoons minced fresh ginger

4 scallions, green stems cut into 1-inch sections

1 package (10 ounces) coleslaw mix (about 4$\frac{1}{2}$ cups)

1$\frac{1}{2}$ cup shredded carrots

$\frac{1}{4}$ cup rice wine or sake

MU SHU SAUCE (combine in a small bowl)

3 tablespoons soy sauce, or to taste

$\frac{1}{4}$ cup rice wine or sake

1 teaspoon sugar

$\frac{1}{4}$ teaspoon freshly ground black pepper

1 teaspoon cornstarch

12 to 16 Mandarin pancakes or flour tortillas, lightly brushed with toasted sesame oil and steamed for 10 minutes

$\frac{3}{4}$ cup hoisin sauce mixed with 2$\frac{1}{2}$ tablespoons water

1. Cut off the stems of the shiitake mushrooms and discard. Trim the stems of the cremini mushrooms. Cut all caps into thin slices.

2. Heat a heavy skillet or a wok over medium-high heat until hot. Add 1 tablespoon of the oil and heat until hot. Add the eggs and salt and stir-fry over high heat to scramble, then remove to a plate or push to one side of the pan.

3. Add the remaining 1 tablespoon oil to the skillet and heat over high heat until hot. Add the Seasonings and stir-fry for 10 seconds, until fragrant. Add the mushrooms and scallion greens and toss lightly for 1½ minutes. Add the coleslaw mix, shredded carrots, and rice wine. Toss lightly, cover, and reduce the heat to medium. Cook for about 3 minutes, uncover, and cook until the vegetables are crisp-tender. Return the egg to the pan and add the Mu Shu Sauce. Toss lightly, stirring to prevent lumps. When the sauce has thickened, scoop the stir-fry onto a platter.

4. To eat, place a hot pancake on a plate, smear a dollop of the hoisin sauce mixture on the wrapper, and spoon the stir-fried mixture on top. Roll up the wrapper, ends tucked in, and eat while hot.

VARIATION: *Replace the scallions with 2 cups shredded garlic chives, leeks, daikon radishes, or broccoli slaw.*

Add 1 pound shredded pork loin, boneless chicken, shrimp, very firm tofu, or top round or flank steak.

Shiitake mushrooms contain lentinan, which has been shown to strengthen the immune system and stop or slow tumor growth. It may also help lower cholesterol.

CHAPTER 8

༄ৡ৾

IRRESISTIBLE SWEETS

IRRESISTIBLE SWEETS

AS A RULE, the Chinese do not traditionally eat what we consider desserts. They usually prefer to finish the meal with a plate of refreshing fruit—and after a multi-course Chinese banquet, who would complain? But since I started my cooking career in my late teens as a pastry chef in a bakery, and then through working in various restaurants and studying with an incredibly talented French pastry chef in Paris, desserts have become a natural part of my repertoire. And I often like at least a bite of something sweet after a not-too filling meal. My husband usually insists on it, and his passion is dark chocolate.

This chapter offers both types of dishes: There are the lighter, fruitier recipes like Spiced Pears in Mulled Cider, Roasted Peaches with Cardamom Whipped Cream, and Baked Apples Layered with Cinnamon Streusel as well as the more sumptuous offerings of Ginger Chocolate-Covered Ice Cream Bonbons and Molten Orange-Chocolate Cupcakes.

The selection of dishes is pretty varied, with many of the recipes created in deference to quick and easy preparation with an emphasis on health. However, having said that, I must admit that I like a rich and slightly extravagant confection every now and then as well as the next person, so I've included a few of those as well.

Whatever you choose to prepare, before you start eating: Take a deep breath, slow down, and savor each bite, treasuring the richness and fully enjoying the experience.

SPICED PEARS IN MULLED CIDER

4 TO 6 SERVINGS

Poaching fruit is effortless, and with this recipe you get two dishes: the fragrant tender pears and the delicious mulled cider. The dessert is particularly satisfying after a heavy meal. Add a dollop of vanilla ice cream or whipped cream, if desired.

POACHING MIXTURE

- 1½ quarts (6 cups) cider or apple juice
- 2 sticks cinnamon, each about 3 inches long
- 3 slices fresh ginger, smashed with the flat side of a knife
- 2 whole cloves
- Peel of 1 tangerine or orange

- 6 slightly underripe Anjou or Bartlett pears
- 1 lemon, cut in half

1. Mix the Poaching Mixture ingredients in a large, nonaluminum pot. Bring to a boil, stirring until the sugar dissolves. Reduce the heat to low and simmer, partially covered, for 15 minutes to infuse the flavors.

2. Meanwhile, peel the pears, leaving the stems on. Rub the surfaces with the lemon halves to prevent them from turning brown. Carefully place the pears in the poaching liquid and squeeze the juice from the lemon into the pot. Bring the liquid to a boil again, then reduce the heat to low. Simmer uncovered until the pears are tender, 25 to 30 minutes. Test by piercing the pears with a knife. Let the pears sit in the liquid for 10 minutes. Using a slotted spoon, transfer the pears to a bowl.

3. Strain the seasonings (orange peel, cinnamon sticks, cloves, and ginger slices) from the poaching mixture and discard. Pour 3 cups of the Poaching Mixture into a heavy saucepan and bring to a boil. Reduce the heat to medium and cook for about 30 minutes, until the sauce is reduced and syrupy. Pour the syrup over the pears. Serve warm, or chill for at least 3 hours with a little syrup and serve cold. The pears can be poached one day ahead and refrigerated, then reheated if desired.

VARIATION: *Substitute firm apples such as Delicious or Granny Smith for the pears.*

The Chinese believe that pears
eliminate heat from the lungs and relieve dryness.

JUICY CANDIED-GINGER ORANGE SLICES

4 TO 6 SERVINGS

One of the fastest and easiest recipes in my dessert repertoire so it has become one of my orange-season favorites. If you are feeling decadent, serve it with vanilla or chocolate ice cream.

5 navel oranges, peeled

¼ cup honey

2 tablespoons chopped candied ginger

1 teaspoon ground cinnamon

1. Cut the oranges into ½-inch slices and place in a bowl. Add the honey, candied ginger, and cinnamon and very carefully mix to coat the slices.

2. Arrange the slices in a large overlapping circle on a dessert platter and let sit for 15 minutes at room temperature. Serve.

Oranges are packed with flavonoids and vitamin C. The pith provides anti-cancer agents and important bioflavonoids. Oranges are also rich in fiber.

BAKED APPLES LAYERED WITH CINNAMON STREUSEL

6 SERVINGS

My son adores my sour cream coffee cake with its cinnamon streusel layers, as well as my apple crisp. Drawing inspiration from the two, I created this dish of baked apples, a satisfying and healthy dessert. Serve them plain, or top with a dollop of Greek yogurt or vanilla ice cream.

6 medium baking apples such as Empire or Delicious

2 lemons, cut in half

STREUSEL (combine in a mixing bowl)

½ cup raisins

½ cup firmly packed light brown sugar

¼ cup granulated sugar

¼ cup unsalted butter, softened to room temperature

1 teaspoon ground cinnamon

½ teaspoon salt

½ cup apple cider or apple juice

1. Preheat the oven to 375°F. Cut a thin slice off the bottom of each apple so it will sit upright, then slice off the top third. Using an apple corer or a melon baller, scoop out the stem, core, and seeds of each apple. Cut the apples in half horizontally, halfway between the top and bottom. Squeeze lemon juice onto the cut surfaces to prevent discoloration. Arrange apples, cavity side up, in a 13 × 9 × 2-inch glass baking dish.

2. Roughly divide the Streusel mixture in 6 portions. Using a spoon or your hands, spread a portion of the streusel evenly over the surface of the cut layers of each apple. Put the halves of each apple back together and arrange in the pan. Pour the cider over and around the apples. Cover the pan securely with aluminum foil, sealing the edges.

3. Bake the apples in the middle of the oven for 20 minutes. Uncover and baste the apples with the juice. Continue baking, basting occasionally, for 10 to 15 minutes, until the apples are tender. Serve warm in some of the juice.

VARIATION: *Replace the apples with pears or pear apples and bake for 35 to 40 minutes, or until tender.*

> In addition to its pleasing flavor, cinnamon fights colds, coughs, and fevers and relieves gas and indigestion.

ROASTED PEACHES WITH CARDAMOM WHIPPED CREAM

6 SERVINGS

Roasting fruit accentuates its ambrosial qualities as well as caramelizes the sugars, so the end result is even more delectable. The cardamom flavor is very subtle and adds another dimension to the dish.

1 cup heavy cream

1½ tablespoons granulated sugar

3 whole cardamom pods, smashed with the flat side of a knife

6 medium ripe, but firm, peaches

2 tablespoons unsalted butter

3 tablespoons light brown sugar

¼ teaspoon five-spice powder or nutmeg

1 teaspoon vanilla extract

1. Mix the heavy cream, granulated sugar, and cardamom pods in a mixing bowl. Cover with plastic wrap and chill for 30 minutes.

2. Preheat the oven to 425°F. Peel, halve, and remove the pits from the peaches. (If you are having difficulties pitting the peaches, leave the pit in and remove after baking.) Arrange the peaches, cut-side up, in a pie or quiche pan. Place the butter in a heatproof ramekin or bowl and microwave on high for 20 to 30 seconds, until melted. Remove and mix with the brown sugar and five-spice powder. Spoon the mixture onto the peaches.

3. Roast the peaches until the sugar bubbles and oozes and the peaches are tender, 15 to 20 minutes. Remove and arrange the peaches in serving bowls. Let cool.

4. Remove the cardamom pods from the cream and discard. Add the vanilla extract to the cream, and, using a hand beater or whisk, whip until stiff. Portion the peaches onto plates or in bowls, spoon a generous dollop of the whipped cream on top, and serve.

VARIATION: *Use nectarines or pears in place of the peaches. Bake for 20 to 25 minutes, until tender.*

Peaches and nectarines are believed to help replenish body fluids and are prescribed by Chinese doctors for dry coughs.

STRAWBERRY AND PLUM WINE GRANITA

6 SERVINGS

Prior to writing this book, I hadn't prepared many granitas. But I've discovered that they are simple, require no special equipment, and are so refreshing and light that now I'm a big fan. Most recipes require you to stir the granita every half hour, but I prefer a slightly lazier version.

1 cup boiling hot water

¾ cup sugar

1 pound strawberries, rinsed and hulled

1 cup plum wine

2 tablespoons fresh lemon juice

1. Stir the hot water with the sugar in a mixing bowl until the sugar dissolves to make a syrup.

2. Cut the strawberries in half and place in the bowl of a food processor. Blend until smooth. Add the syrup, plum wine, and lemon juice and continue processing.

3. Pour the mixture into a 13 × 9 × 2-inch nonaluminum or glass baking pan. Freeze for about 1½ hours. Using a fork, stir the icy portions into the middle of the pan. Continue freezing for about 30 minutes. Using a fork, scrape the granita into flaky crystals, spoon into bowls, and serve. To keep in the freezer for at least 1½ weeks, cover securely with plastic wrap.

CREAMY LEMON-VANILLA YOGURT WITH BLUEBERRIES

4 TO 6 SERVINGS

Since her very first book, *Flavours,* Australian cookbook author Donna Hay's easy and enticing recipes have inspired me. Just a glance through *New Food Fast* or *No Time to Cook* fuels my imagination for new recipes. Such is the case with the recipe below.

2 cups plain Greek yogurt

¼ cup honey

1½ tablespoons finely grated lemon zest

1 teaspoon vanilla extract

1 pint blueberries, rinsed and drained

1. In a mixing bowl, mix the yogurt, honey, lemon zest, and vanilla extract until well blended. Chill for 15 minutes.

2. Spoon the yogurt into serving bowls and sprinkle liberally with the blueberries. Alternatively, create alternating layers of blueberries and yogurt as in a parfait. Serve cold.

VARIATIONS: *Substitute any type of cut fruit for the blueberries, including peaches or other berries like raspberries, blackberries, or strawberries.*

You may also use nonfat yogurt for a lighter, but no less delicious, recipe.

Yogurt contains live bacteria, such as lactobacillus, that are probiotic and essential to maintaining a healthy balance. They boost the immune system and keep the digestive system running smoothly. In addition, the protein in yogurt is easily absorbed by the body, providing it with amino acids needed to build cells.

EASY COCONUT RICE PUDDING
WITH FRESH MANGOES

4 TO 6 SERVINGS

Rice pudding is one of the most delicious mommy foods. I've discovered that you can reduce the preparation time enormously by using precooked rice. Made with the combination of light coconut milk and half-and-half, this rice pudding will certainly draw raves. The broiled mango is a lovely counterpoint, but it can be omitted.

1 cup cooked basmati rice

1 can (15 ounces) light unsweetened coconut milk, stirred well

1/2 cup half-and-half

1/4 cup granulated sugar

1/4 teaspoon freshly ground nutmeg

1/4 teaspoon salt

1 teaspoon vanilla extract

3 ripe mangoes, rinsed and drained

2 tablespoons unsalted butter, melted

1 1/2 tablespoons light brown sugar

1. Bring the rice, coconut milk, half-and-half, granulated sugar, nutmeg, and salt to a boil in a 3- to 4-quart heavy saucepan. Reduce the heat to medium and cook, stirring occasionally, for 8 to 10 minutes, until thickened. Remove from the heat and stir in the vanilla extract. Pour into a serving bowl or individual ramekins.

2. Preheat the broiler. Line a baking pan with aluminum foil.

3. While the rice is cooking, prepare the mangos: Stand a mango upright on one of the pointed ends. Cut off the two fleshy cheeks on the sides, cutting as close to the pit as possible. Score or cut the flesh into 1/4-inch dice, leaving the flesh attached to the skin. Repeat with the remaining mangoes. Place each mango on the baking pan scored side up. Mix the melted butter with the brown sugar and brush on the surface of each scored mango half. Arrange on the prepared pan and broil for 5 minutes, until the brown sugar bubbles.

4. Arrange the mango halves on a plate, or next to each ramekin of warm rice pudding, and serve.

GINGER CHOCOLATE-COVERED ICE CREAM BONBONS

MAKES 12 OR 13 BONBONS

My son and husband have always loved the chocolate-covered ice cream bonbons served at Legal Sea Foods. This is my homage. They are so easy to make, and they make people swoon. I find Ghirardelli, Valrhona, and Callebaut to be the best coating chocolates.

1 pint vanilla ice cream

2 bars (4 ounces each) bittersweet dark chocolate with at least 56 percent cocoa content

¼ cup candied ginger, finely chopped

10-inch bamboo skewers (2 or more)

1. Line a 7- or 8-inch cake pan with waxed paper and chill in the freezer on a level surface. Fill a glass with cold water. Microwave the ice cream on high for 10 seconds and, using a 2-ounce ice cream scoop or a melon baller, shape the ice cream into balls, dipping the scoop in the cold water between each ball. Arrange the ice cream on the chilled pan lined with waxed paper and freeze until firm, about 35 minutes.

2. Smash one of the chocolate bars on a hard surface, breaking it into small pieces. Melt the chocolate over low heat in a double boiler. Add half the chopped ginger and mix thoroughly.

3. Grasping a bamboo skewer in each hand, poke into a frozen ice cream ball and dip the ball in the chocolate, coating completely. Place back on the waxed paper. Repeat to coat half of the balls, then return to the freezer.

4. Clean out the double boiler and repeat the process with the other chocolate bar, the remaining ginger, and the ice cream balls. (If you try to do all the balls in one batch, the chocolate will need to be reheated and might seize.)

VARIATIONS: *Use other flavorings in place of the candied ginger, such as 2 tablespoons of finely grated orange zest or 2 tablespoons Grand Marnier or other liqueur. Replace the vanilla ice cream with other flavors like coffee, strawberry, mango, or dulce de leche.*

Dark chocolate and cocoa are packed
with natural antioxidants.

GINGERY NECTARINE CRISP
WITH SPICED OATMEAL TOPPING

6-8 SERVINGS

Some people are chocoholics. You could call me a crisp-oholic. Take any fruit that's in season, cover it with a cinnamon crisp topping and serve it with a dollop of vanilla ice cream and I am in heaven. Nectarines tend to be less mealy than peaches so I find them preferable.

TOPPING

- ¾ cup unbleached all-purpose flour
- ¾ cup quick-cooking oats
- ½ cup sugar
- ½ cup lightly packed light brown sugar
- 1 teaspoon cinnamon
- ½ teaspoon salt
- ½ cup (1 stick) cold, unsalted butter, cut into ½-inch pieces

FRUIT FILLING

- 3 pounds firm, but almost ripe nectarines (about 10)
- 1 lemon, cut in half
- ⅓ cup light brown sugar
- ½ teaspoon ground cinnamon
- 1½ tablespoons cornstarch
- 2½ tablespoons finely minced candied ginger

1½ tablespoons unsalted butter for greasing the pan

1. Preheat the oven to 375°F.

2. To make the Topping, put the flour, oats, brown sugar, and salt in a food processor fitted with a steel blade. Add the butter pieces and pulse, turning the machine on and off, until the mixture resembles cornmeal. Set aside. Alternatively, you may make the topping in a bowl, using a pastry blender or a knife, cutting the cold butter into the dry ingredients.

3. To make the Fruit Filling, peel the nectarines, cut in half, core, and rub with the cut lemon. Squeeze any remaining juice in with the nectarines. Cut the halves into ¾-inch thick slices and toss lightly in the cinnamon, sugar and candied ginger in a bowl. Generously grease a 9-inch square baking dish (preferably ceramic or glass) or a 10-inch diameter round pie dish with high sides. Pour the nectarines into the prepared pan. Spoon the topping over the nectarines, sprinkling it evenly.

4. Bake about 1 hour until the crumb topping is golden with a few spots of light brown, and the filling is bubbling. Let cool slightly before serving warm or at room temperature. To reheat, bake uncovered in a preheated 300°F oven for 10 to 15 minutes until hot.

VARIATION: *Reduce the amount of nectarines to 1¾ pounds and add 1 pint or 2 cups of fresh blueberries or 1½ pints of fresh raspberries.*

MOLTEN ORANGE-CHOCOLATE CUPCAKES

MAKES 6 CUPCAKES

These sumptuous cakes are firm on the edges and liquid in the center. You can prepare them hours or a day in advance and bake them at the last minute. For the best result, use a high-quality dark chocolate such as Valrhona or Callebaut, usually sold in chunks in supermarkets.

6 tablespoons unsalted butter, softened to room temperature

2 tablespoons unsweetened cocoa, for dusting cupcake tins

8 ounces bittersweet chocolate

⅓ cup granulated sugar

3 large eggs

1 large egg yolk

1 teaspoon vanilla extract

Finely grated zest of 2 navel oranges (about 2 tablespoons)

⅓ cup all-purpose flour

½ teaspoon salt

Confectioners' sugar for dusting

1. Preheat the oven to 400°F. Melt 2 tablespoons of the butter and use to generously grease 6 cups of a muffin tin or 6 soufflé dishes, then dust with the cocoa powder.

2. Melt the chocolate over low heat in a double boiler. Cream the remaining 4 tablespoons butter and the granulated sugar in a small electric mixer or a food processor fitted with a steel blade. Add the eggs one at a time and then the egg yolk, beating vigorously after each addition. Add the vanilla extract and orange zest, then the flour and salt and beat or process until just mixed. Add the melted chocolate and beat or process until just mixed. Divide the batter among the prepared cupcake tins or soufflé dishes. (If preparing ahead, cover with plastic wrap and chill. Bring to room temperature before baking.)

3. Bake the cakes for 13 to 15 minutes, until the edges are puffed and slightly cracked and the very middle is still soft and jiggles when lightly shaken. Let sit for 5 minutes. If using cupcake tins, run a knife or a spatula around the edges and turn out onto individual plates. Sprinkle the tops with the confectioners' sugar and serve.

VARIATION: *For mocha cupcakes, omit the orange zest or replace it with ¼ cup espresso or strong coffee.*

CRISP-TOASTED ALMOND WONTON CRISPS

MAKES 100 SMALL CRISPS

Serve these simple wonton triangles by themselves, with tea, or with sliced fruit and/or ice cream or sorbet. They can be prepared in advance, stored in resealable zipper storage bags, and re-crisped in a 350°F oven before serving.

2 tablespoons virgin olive oil, or olive oil spray

1½ cups sliced almonds

¼ cup sugar

2 teaspoons ground cinnamon

1 egg white, lightly beaten

2 tablespoons maple syrup

50 wonton wrappers

1. Preheat the oven to 425°F. Brush or spray 2 baking sheets with olive oil.

2. Put the almonds in a plastic bag and, using a rolling pin or the bottom of a heavy pan, crush coarsely.

3. In a bowl, mix the crushed almonds with the sugar and cinnamon. Toss lightly to mix. In another bowl, mix the beaten egg white with the maple syrup.

4. Arrange the wonton wrappers side by side on the prepared baking sheets and brush their surfaces with the egg white mixture. Sprinkle the almond cinnamon mixture on top. Cut in half diagonally into triangles, using a sharp pizza cutter or a chef's knife. Bake for 5 to 6 minutes, until golden brown. Remove with a spatula to a cooling rack and let sit until cool. Arrange on a serving dish or serve with individual portions of cut fruit, ice cream, or sorbet.

CANDIED GINGER SNAPS

MAKES ABOUT 30 COOKIES

The combination of candied ginger and ground ginger (plus a few other spices) gives these cookies their delicious and unique flavor. Decorate the tops with chopped or shredded candied ginger or large crystal sugar. They keep beautifully in a tightly sealed container for a week, or in the freezer. After defrosting, you can quickly recrisp them in a 350°F oven for 5 minutes.

1¾ cups all-purpose flour

1½ teaspoons ground ginger

1½ teaspoons ground cinnamon

¼ teaspoon allspice

¼ teaspoon baking soda

½ cup (1 stick) unsalted butter, softened
    to room temperature

½ cup firmly packed light brown sugar

¼ cup molasses

1 large egg

¼ cup minced candied ginger

½ cup granulated sugar

¼ cup shredded or chopped candied
    ginger (for garnish)

1. Sift together the flour, ginger, cinnamon, allspice, and baking soda.

2. In a mixing bowl with an electric mixer, beat the butter and brown sugar until light and fluffy, about 5 minutes. Add the molasses, egg, and minced ginger and mix. Gradually add the flour mixture and mix to form a rough dough. Turn the dough out onto a lightly floured surface and shape into a circle. Wrap in plastic wrap and refrigerate for at least 2 hours until firm, or overnight.

3. Preheat the oven to 375°F. Lightly butter 2 baking sheets. Scoop out one level tablespoon of the dough and roll into a ball. Roll in the granulated sugar to coat and place on the prepared baking sheet. Repeat with the remaining dough, leaving 2 inches between each cookie. Dipping the bottom of a glass in the sugar, press each ball with the glass into a 2-inch circle. Sprinkle the tops with the shredded or chopped ginger.

4. Bake the cookies for 10 to 12 minutes, rotating the sheets after 4 minutes to ensure even baking. The tops should be golden. Let the cookies cool slightly and carefully transfer to wire racks to cool.

> Ginger soothes nausea, aids circulation, and is antibacterial—
> medicinal properties that have been acknowledged by
> Chinese doctors for centuries, and are now accepted
> in the Western medical community.

ACKNOWLEDGMENTS

This book grew out of conversations with other cooks and former students, all of whom have grappled with the daily challenge of preparing a delicious, healthy, and quick dinner every night for themselves and their families, a duty I also undertake on a daily basis. They inspired me to develop many of the recipes, tips, and strategies that are presented in these pages. Fortunately, as with my other books, I was lucky to have a host of additional people who helped, inspired, and collaborated, and I would like to thank the following:

The legion of chefs and home cooks in the United States, Europe, and Asia whose food stimulated my palate and nurtured creativity during my travels here and abroad.

Superb cooks in their own right and ace recipe testers, my treasured buddies, most notably Debby Richards and Françoise Fetchko repeatedly helped me refine the recipes in this book. In addition, I'd like to thank my indispensable "wives," assistants Jennifer Saphier Whitman and Amy Takeuchi, who not only helped recipe-test, but provided assistance in dealing with the often overwhelming chores in my and my husband's daily life. Artists/designers Julie Lutts and Ruth Bauer, both dear friends, were very helpful with cover support.

I would be remiss not to give a special thank-you to Roger Berkowitz, Ida Faber, and Joan Giblin at Legal Seafoods, all of whom have been incredibly generous and supportive as an underwriting sponsor for www.SpicesofLife.com, my food/health/lifestyle Web site and video blogs. I'd also like to tip my hat to my past and present videographers: Steve Garfield, Haley Hao, Dave Ells, Elissa Mintz, Sasha Goldberg, and Marcella Hoekstra. My terrific editor at *The Daily*

Beast, Jane Frye, has also been an enthusiastic fan and my great pal. *GourmetLive* editor Kemp Minifie and Epicurious.com editor-in-chief Tanya Steel have also been wonderful supporters.

I have been especially fortunate in my book ventures to have had great editors and associates who have brought my work to life. This book is no different. First and foremost, I'd like to thank Pam Krauss, my innovative and visionary editor who first saw the potential and then became a fierce advocate for *Simple Asian Meals*. Her assistant Victoria Glerum also helped a great deal. I was equally thrilled to work with art director Christina Gaugler, whose exquisite design shaped this book. Chris is not only talented, but she is a dream to work with. Her calm demeanor and discerning eye proved to be a remarkably helpful asset at the photo shoot and her judgment never wavered, despite her grueling schedule and commuting every day from Pennsylvania to New York City.

I would be hard-pressed to fully express my gratitude and thanks to Romulo Yanes and his assistants "Critter" Knutsen, Andrew Katzowitz, and Patrick Marinello. I have been a huge fan of Romulo's extraordinary work since his earliest days at *Gourmet* and he is one of the most generous, kind, and patient photographers I have worked with. But Romulo was just part of the team who helped create the truly exquisite photos for this book. Paul Grimes, stylist extraordinaire, meticulous selector of ingredients, and phenomenal cook, worked his magic with the aid of John Bjostad, Diana Perez, and Josh Israel. I have never seen anyone more talented than Paul at coaxing food to look so beautiful and delicious at the same time. Thanks, too, to Paige Hicks (and her assistant Nidia Cueva), another indispensable member of the photography team, whose amazing array of props and surfaces made the photos especially beautiful.

Jane Dystel, my fantastic agent and friend, has been a stalwart cheerleader, advisor, and champion for the past 12 years and I have really appreciated her counsel. Her partner, Miriam Goderich, and their staff have also become like family, so I would sincerely like to send a big thank-you and hug their way.

I am particularly lucky to have so many generous and wonderful friends, family, and former students all over the country and world who have nurtured and cheered me on through all of my endeavors. Thanks and a big kiss to you all.

But my biggest "thank-yous" are reserved for my sweetheart and loving husband, Don, and the son who makes us so proud, Jesse; they continue to make my life joyful, fun, and memorable. I am truly blessed!

Nina Simonds
June 2011

INDEX

Underscored page references indicate boxed text or sidebars. **Boldfaced** page references indicate photographs.

Conversion Chart

These equivalents have been slightly rounded to make measuring easier.

Volume Measurements

U.S.	Imperial	Metric
¼ tsp	–	1 ml
½ tsp	–	2 ml
1 tsp	–	5 ml
1 Tbsp	–	15 ml
2 Tbsp (1 oz)	1 fl oz	30 ml
¼ cup (2 oz)	2 fl oz	60 ml
⅓ cup (3 oz)	3 fl oz	80 ml
½ cup (4 oz)	4 fl oz	120 ml
⅔ cup (5 oz)	5 fl oz	160 ml
¾ cup (6 oz)	6 fl oz	180 ml
1 cup (8 oz)	8 fl oz	240 ml

Weight Measurements

U.S.	Metric
1 oz	30 g
2 oz	60 g
4 oz (¼ lb)	115 g
5 oz (⅓ lb)	145 g
6 oz	170 g
7 oz	200 g
8 oz (½ lb)	230 g
10 oz	285 g
12 oz (¾ lb)	340 g
14 oz	400 g
16 oz (1 lb)	455 g
2.2 lb	1 kg

Length Measurements

U.S.	Metric
¼"	0.6 cm
½"	1.25 cm
1"	2.5 cm
2"	5 cm
4"	11 cm
6"	15 cm
8"	20 cm
10"	25 cm
12" (1')	30 cm

Pan Sizes

U.S.	Metric
8" cake pan	20 × 4 cm sandwich or cake tin
9" cake pan	23 × 3.5 cm sandwich or cake tin
11" × 7" baking pan	28 × 18 cm baking tin
13" × 9" baking pan	32.5 × 23 cm baking tin
15" × 10" baking pan	38 × 25.5 cm baking tin (Swiss roll tin)
1½ qt baking dish	1.5 liter baking dish
2 qt baking dish	2 liter baking dish
2 qt rectangular baking dish	30 × 19 cm baking dish
9" pie plate	22 × 4 or 23 × 4 cm pie plate
7" or 8" springform pan	18 or 20 cm springform or loose-bottom cake tin
9" × 5" loaf pan	23 × 13 cm or 2 lb narrow loaf tin or pâté tin

Temperatures

Fahrenheit	Centigrade	Gas
140°	60°	–
160°	70°	–
180°	80°	–
225°	105°	¼
250°	120°	½
275°	135°	1
300°	150°	2
325°	160°	3
350°	180°	4
375°	190°	5
400°	200°	6
425°	220°	7
450°	230°	8
475°	245°	9
500°	260°	–